COYOTE HUNTING

FARM STYLE

TAKE TWO

BLOW A CROW DROP A YOTE!

SHERI BAITY

ISBN: 978-1-962402-36-1

Contact the author:

570-916-5475

sheribaity@yahoo.com

@Crows-Nest-Calls

TABLE OF CONTENTS

ACKNOWLEDGEMENTS

I would like to Thank My Dad for teaching me, no matter how hard things get in life to "Never Give Up" and also to "Stand in My Truth." I have been very Proud to carry that through my life, in his honor. You never gave up on me Dad! Although you have left this world now, you live on forever in my heart and mind! I am so Blessed!!!

Thank You goes 30-plus years to My Husband. We have seen our highs and lows in life but time showed that no matter what, you stood by me as we held each other up. You are my Rock, my love and a beat of my heart. I say we go another 30 plus years together. I would be lost without you in this world! I Love You Mr. Baity!!!

To My Daughter, in spite of the life you started out on, because of me, you are my Biggest Success Story. Thank You for allowing me to go along on your journey with you! Also Thank You for being my cheerleader even when I felt I didn't have any cheer left in me some days. For your help on writing proposals and speeches from time to time were more appreciated then I ever expressed properly. I am so Proud of You!!

To My Beautiful Ba-Bay, My Granddaughter... where to start with you, my Lil Red Winged Blackbird. Watching you grow up has been the sweetest pleasure of my entire life. From your growth, to the changes, to seeing you find your life purpose to becoming a young woman has been incredible. Thank You for letting me into your world and of course the technical help from time to time to this computer challenged person! Don't ever give up your Daydreams! Keep reaching and grabbing onto each and every star! You Deserve It! I am so very Proud of You!!!

And last but not least... To the Court Jester, my son in law. Thank You for bringing free comedy to this family and wrapping everything up perfectly! You have been the topic of many conversations. I will leave that up to your own interpretations... lol. The constant Love and balance you give to my daughter and granddaughter is Beautiful and warming for my heart to see. I appreciate you more then I say. Thank You for being there for the girls and completing the family!

CHAPTER 1

I COULD NEVER HAVE IMAGINED

"Dreams are possible,
passions are made to become reality,
and stories of 30-plus years are designed to share!"

I am still learning from the many animals that I both observe and hunt. Fascinating in so many spectrums that amaze me. I follow the winged ones listening to their vocalizations, watching their wing dances as they fly and learning their chatter as they soar above warning others of the dangers below. I call them Messengers of the Forest. It quickly grabs my attention to be on alert as I grab my binoculars.

Five hundred yards away at my crow's attention, I see a coyote setting in the corner of the swamp. I silently send a message to the crows to bring him closer so that I can make an accurate shot. Two fly down from the tree top at about 225 yards in the clearing and start cawing loudly. One starts flopping as if its wing is broken. Then they Caw even more while the one crow is still faking its injury.

The coyote's interest is peaked and stands up, listening with great curiosity. The crows do their act for another 2 minutes or so as the coyote slowly makes his way towards the crows. He stops momentarily as he positions himself to make a quick lunge towards the crows for an easy meal. With a quick movement, the crows fly up in the air and do wing dances above him cawing nonstop.

He sits down again, but thanks to the crows he is much closer now. Definitely within my shooting range now. The crows land again a little closer to me and proceed with their script of cawing and broken wing dancing.

The coyote slowly creeps towards them for another attempt at that free meal. As he lunges again, the crows take flight. Again, the coyote is left without food. With the crows in the air and the coyote standing still I take the opportunity to make my shot.

I get him in my site and slowly squeeze the trigger of my .243. One shot just behind the front shoulders and the coyote drops.

The crows are all around now doing wing dances above the coyote. I caw back to them, giving Thanks for their help.

When I make it to the coyote, the crows are silently perched in the tree tops around me. I grab a hand full of nuts I had in my hunting bag and toss it in the air. I also grab a piece of beef jerky and place it by the mouth of the coyote for blessings of Thanks.

This has always been my way. I will never change that. It is, to me, what I have learned and live by. After picking up the coyote it is time to head back to the farm and weigh him up. I already checked the sex before I picked him up. A nice male coming in at 35lbs. I take a few pictures and share the story with my family or anyone that wants to listen. It's time for me now to Retreat, Reflect, Pray, and Give Thanks to God Above.

People always ask me how I call them in…sometimes no calling is needed. Some days it is just a feeling that I need to go and where I need to be. But sometimes it is where the crows are telling me to be as I watch them alert me to take down another trouble maker on my farm that needs to go.

I don't hunt crows but I use the crows to be my eyes and ears many times in coyote hunting. I also give them a haven on my farm. No Crow hunting is allowed on our 225 acres of land. They will always have that guarantee from me.

I also pay attention to the woodpeckers and blue jays as well. When they sound off their alarm tones, I also pay attention to where they are vocalizing from and flying away from.

I have learned so much about hunting just by watching all animals. They have taught me more in the 30 years of hunting that no book, article or show could ever teach me. When they speak, show their body language or movement… I watch and learn. I will forever be grateful for their teachings.

CHAPTER 2

DADDY, I COULD SEE HIS BREATH

I was four hours away from home, but it would be days before I could get a chance to see my loved ones. Two and a half months of living out of my suitcase and only going home for three to four days at a time was starting to wear on me. The sign said New York City 52 miles. I had to laugh to myself over that one. I was in the mountains of Middletown, New York, so close to the Big Apple, but I had no desire to go the distance.

was on my way to take two fathers and their son's coyote hunting. I gave the guys a choice. I said, "Boys, I'm getting tired. You have a choice. You can either go out hunting tonight at 11 p.m., on this full moon night or you can get up early and go out at 5 a.m. tomorrow morning." Thank Goodness they opted for tonight. My plan was to get this done and when I got up in the morning, I was finally headed home.

I had a good feeling about this night. Full moon has always been the best time to vocalize with coyotes. It has been like a special bonding time, a meeting of the minds, so to speak, between the coyotes and myself. After all, the last coyote I shot was during a full moon on New Year's Eve, so the odds were good.

My entourage was John Sr., John Jr., Phil and son Zach. The boys were both thirteen. Looking into their eyes, they were eager to listen and participate. I saw in them remarkable young men with hopes and dreams.

Heading out on the gator, the temperature was near twenty degrees. There was not a breeze in the air and the stars just beamed as the moon illuminated our way up into an old mining site. I already knew I was going to go down in the bowl or the pit to do my calling. It would be a great place to resonate the sounds that I would be making. I put Phil and his son Zach just outside of the old mine shaft. From all signs, it looked like this was the coyotes den site. To the right of me, about 200 yards around the bend, was a gravel mound in the bottom of the pit. The gravel mound stretched about 20 feet wide at the top and stood around 25 feet high. John Sr and John Jr took each side of the top of the mound.

Coyote tracks were everywhere I looked, showing up clearly in the four-inch-deep blanket of snow. With the moons rays it was practically daylight. I waited for another 15 minutes of silence before I started calling. In all directions just inside the woods that surrounded the pit I was in, I could hear footsteps, but couldn't see exactly where they were coming from. It was eerie in a way, but thrilling in other ways. My adrenaline was pumped.

Since rabbit distress sounds work well with coyotes in New York, I pulled out my call and went into a short dying rabbit series. Then I pulled up my closed reed and barked off in a different direction. I turned my head again and came out with two chirps, simulating a female coyote answering the bark. Then I started growling with my closed reed and barked and growled some more. I pulled up my open reed and started yelping as if a coyote was in a fight and had just been bitten. I then went into more barking, growling and yelping, ending with a very short bark. This whole scenario continued about one minute. I let the silence fall into the air and listened. Barks and aggressive footsteps were coming closer, but still no visual for me.

I soaked up the noises for about four minutes: these sounds in the silence can be so exhilarating and have so much beauty in them. After waiting, I produced another sound. The Old Man in the Moon was smiling down on me right above my head. I gave him a smiling wink and went back to another calling scenario for any possible takers. Things were hot, I could feel it. People sometimes ask me how I know when there is a coyote in the area, it's just a feeling I get that can't be explained with words.

I picked up the open reed and let out a deep, resonating lone howl. Barking responses were heard and then the pack started lighting up with yip howls, lone howls, barking and anything else they had in their vocabulary. There was nothing else to do now but join in, and join in I certainly did. I was now a member of their choir. I was completely surrounded by the coyotes. It was virtually impossible for me to count just how many coyotes were there responding. The next 30 seconds of silence seemed like five minutes. More scurrying of footsteps and then I hear it...

The most beautiful low toned howl came from the direction of the mineshaft where Phil and Zach were positioned. I came to find out later that two coyotes had come up behind them. The bigger of the two coyotes was the one doing the howling. Zach had the howling coyotes in his sights, but couldn't pull the hammer back on his gun. His gloves were too thick and he just couldn't manipulate the hammer to make the shot. His Father said that he should have put the extension on the hammer before they left because there wasn't much clearance between the hammer and scope. When the coyotes saw him fumbling, they took off. Zach and his Dad were so excited and scared at the same time.

Phil told me later that it was the closest he had ever been to a coyote. Then he told me of the thrill that his son experienced. He said that his son had leaned into him and said, "Daddy... I could see his breath!!!"

I tried a few more series of calls to see if there were any remaining coyotes but there were no takers. I called it an evening, playing my normal taps on the open reed call. Everyone came down to the pit with their stories and then I found out what happened with John Sr and John Jr.

John said that when all the coyotes came in, two were circling around the bottom of the gravel mound. The brush was too thick around the bottom, so they couldn't get a shot. He said when they came in, it took no time at all before he and his son were back to back, rather than 20 feet apart. John Sr said, "I thought my son was going to jump right in my lap, he was so scared…and so was I!! We just kept tight to each other, hoping you would stop calling really quick!!"

I grinned and laughed, then told them, "Well boys, I didn't hear any shots or screaming, so I figured it was alright for me to keep on calling." We loaded up the gator and headed back to John's house. On our way out, we took a detour and drove by the gravel mound where John Sr and John Jr had been hunting. Sure enough, there were two fresh sets of coyote tracks circling the mound.

So, there you have it. No coyotes were harmed in the making of this story, but it will go down in my memory as one of the best hunts ever! Sunday morning came around and I was heading home with a smile on face. The words I kept hearing with each mile I drove were, "DADDY I COULD SEE HIS BREATH!!!"

CHAPTER 3

MY FIRST COYOTE,
WHERE IT ALL STARTED

It was my second year of hunting but my first year of getting anything. December 1993 was the time. My husband had purchased a gun for me. There would be no more borrowing a gun from the family. This was my first ever. I think that all happened because I had made a pitch to my husband that the reason I came home empty handed the first year of hunting was because I didn't have a gun of my own. It certainly wasn't because I didn't put in the time

He gave in quite nicely and I ended up with a Winchester Model 70 XTR .243. Great weight and virtually no kick. I had a gunsmith cut three inches off of the stock and put a nice recoil pad on. That took quite a bit of convincing from my part. The man just kept on telling me that he had never cut that much off of a gun and maybe I only needed an inch off. After putting my foot down and showing him that I needed three inches by pulling it up and trying to reach the trigger, he caved in and did as I asked. The results were sheer perfection.

I had a 3x9 Tasco scope mounted on and bought a beautiful leather strap with turkeys stamped that were painted. I was all set. My sales pitch to my husband must have been good. The first day of fall turkey I came hiking down the steep pasture carrying the biggest gobbler ever killed in the family. I still hold the title to this day.

The first morning of buck was quite uneventful. About 10 a.m., 7 deer came running out of the swamp, up the hill towards me. The first five were doe but the sixth was a three point, all on one antler. I admit, I had the proverbial "buck fever" and totally blew the shot. A neighbor about 2 miles straight down the fields got him shortly later. After that, only doe were running by. There were lots of shots around me though, which only meant the bucks were headed elsewhere.

My confidence was at an all-time low. I kept on thinking back about my first year. All the shooting I had done in the past resulting in nothing to show, was a constant thought in my mind. So, I started talking to myself aloud, "Come over my way bucks. I can't hit anything today. You are totally safe around me!" I'm sure we've all had those moments in hunting at some point in time. And if we haven't, well then, I had them for you all. The temps were extremely frigid and I was frustrated and hungry. So, it was back to the house to warm up and fuel up and of course whine. And whine I did.

At 1 p.m., a neighbor of ours, Dale came down. Dale was the same guy that helped me sight in my new scope and he also gave me pointers about aiming and squeeze the trigger, never pull it. He told us to grab our stuff, that some guys were going to walk the woods and maybe we would get lucky and get a deer.

My husband, Gary was all excited. I kind of laughed to myself. Out of ALL the times the woods were driven, we ALWAYS ended up home, empty handed. Furthermore, after missing in the morning, let's just say my confidence level was low.

We loaded up in my husband's truck and up through the fields we went. The plan was, they were going to drop me off on one hill where my cabin now sits and they would be over on the other one across the valley. I was supposed to shoot anything that they might possibly miss. I didn't want to tell them that their plan was awful and totally nerve racking for me because I was new to this. So, I got out of the truck and stood where I was supposed to.

My heart was racing. All I thought was how I couldn't possibly let them down. I needed to do this. Here I am standing all by myself, no gun rest, no cover, wondering what have I got myself into now. Over on their hill, they stood... They had gun rests, cover and loaded with many, many years of hunting experience.

After only a few minutes, all of a sudden, the shooting started from them. They must have emptied their guns at least two times.

I'm over here panicking, thinking I'm in trouble now. I can't even see this buck they are shooting at. They are going to be so mad because I can't find it to shoot it. I quickly glance over to them and see them over their shooting and pointing that something is headed my way. Then they start hollering, "Shoot It, Shoot It! It's coming right to you!!!"

I'm thinking, *Yeah sure guys. Why don't one of you come over here and show me where it is? Maybe then I will shoot it.* Those thoughts no sooner passed and I saw IT running full force through the valley and up the field to me.

The adrenaline immediately kicked in. Everything seemed to be in slow motion. Where the sudden belt of confidence came from, I'll never know. Like a Pro would have done, I found the coyote in my scope. I don't think it could have run any faster than it was at that moment. I pointed the scope ahead of it and waited for it to get into view again. The instant the coyote's nose came into view through the scope, holding my breath I squeezed the trigger. I had just lead my first animal. And it was a success.

The guys over on the other hill were almost comical. I heard Dale happily scream and clapping his hands and Gary excitedly asking "Did she get it? Did she get IT?" Then they heard the sound of the shot finally reach them. Dale had seen the coyote drop so he knew right away. Gary just saw it disappear and wasn't sure.

So to answer their question, I let out one helluva scream and danced a little jig. They were back in their truck and on their way over. Me, on the other hand, seemed to be in a daze still. I was shaking so badly. I think it was half adrenaline rush and half freezing cold.

I pulled my gun up again and looked just to make sure this really happened. And then two more times just to make sure I was sure. The guys got here and we went to see just what I got.

Sure enough, a female coyote, 37 pounds with one shot. We get back down to the farm and another neighbor shows up. He tells us that he watched the whole thing happen from his hill. He was so excited and told me that he was proud of me. The rest of the afternoon was filled with people coming to see the coyote they heard I got. Dale and Gary filled them ALL in with play by play action.

Very few people around here have gotten a coyote and never with one shot. They have always been at least 4 or more shots because they are such strong creatures and too quick to get a vital shot. To my knowledge, there have never been any dead run hits either. So then the nicknames started… Sure Shot, Dead Eye, One Shot, Coyote Woman and Coyote Slayer.

For so long, hunting has been mostly male oriented. To be recognized in this circle of people is great. It's equally nice to be respected for my hunting abilities. It's a great high in my life.

CHAPTER 4

WILCOX, ARIZONA, 2005

I will never forget that trip for the rest of my life. I had the opportunity to camp in the desert for four days with the most elite and experienced predator hunters. They are the best of the best in so many ways. The wealth of knowledge in the years they have under their belts would blow anyone's mind. I was the only east coaster invited to share camp. I was also the only female as well. And when I say camp... I mean camp, not for the glampers out there or for the weak of heart. No running water, no showers, a porta potty with a makeshift shower curtain to give some kind of concealment or privacy. Baby wipes were my only source of a shower. And we were right next to the Mexico border, which was a bit unsettling.

Huntmasters Crew

had been told by a little birdie of the group that the men were a bit ruffled about the fact that they would have to share a camp with a woman. They were told to make sure that they watched their language and act with respect given to the Lady. Well, well… they don't know me very well. I used to be a nighttime dock supervisor for a trucking company. I have seen and heard it all, right down to the time that one of the guys placed a condom on my Garfield's tail! I was always considered just one of the guys. So, I came up with a plan to really make them worry when they saw me.

I went to my hairdresser and had her bleach my hair really blonde. I had my nails manicured to perfection in pink frost. I found a pair of pink camo pants and a pink tank top to go along with the pants. I fully did up my makeup including pink frosted lips. I was READY as I took my flight.

My Buddy picked me up at the airport. I wish ya'll could have seen the look on his face! It was priceless! I of course burst out laughing as I told him my plan to get the guys to relax and lighten up a bit. He was so excited to watch this play out!

We pull up at camp. It was so hot there and I was thankful that I had this lightweight pink camo on. Trying to keep a good poker face while meeting the guys was really hard to do. The guys were all so sickening sweet and well-mannered as they showed me to my tent carrying my luggage and all. I grabbed a bottle of water and got settled in for a few. They told me to meet at the food wagon when I was ready.

I had bought at Spencer's a male, anatomically correct water bottle. I got it filled with ice cold water and hid it behind my back as I walked up to the guys all sitting around. As soon as I took a sip of water and placed it on the table, the guys knew that I had put on the greatest show ever and got them all!!! Oh, the laughter that commenced!!! It was just what I had hoped for! The worries and tension disappeared! Now we could focus on Predator Hunting.

The joke about the men was that the coyotes out west would not understand my calls with the east coast accent! I took it in stride and that just gave me a little more fuel for the fire. Every stand that we went on I chose to do most of the calling. It worked every time as anywhere from two to 4 coyotes would come to my call. They were amazed. I told them it was because of my accent and my pink camo that the coyotes could not resist me! So, even though I had no facilities to wash my clothes out there in the desert, I was told to wear my pink camo for every stand until the trip ended… and so I did!

The coyotes were either really dumb out there or I was just that good at calling. Either way, I called the most coyotes in the camp. I did finally take a stand as shooter. I couldn't miss an opportunity to have a western coyote under my belt.

The food wagon was so dang good! A huge selection of eats from meats being smoked to breakfast to vegetables and always tons of great stories from everyone! I would love nothing more than to name drop here with these men, but won't out of respect for them.

I faced a lot of my fears while on this trip. My fears were scorpions, rattle snakes, tarantulas and killer bees. I conquered them all in just a short time. That was good for me to overcome and learn how to deal with each and every fear that has been bottled up inside me for so long. I am proud that I accomplished this.

It was time for me to head home. I needed to get to the hotel to catch my flight the following morning. We took a group pic, with me in my pink camo of course. The guys were all in agreement that if they were to have any more camp gatherings that they promised to all wear Pink Camo!!! It was sad in a way that in just a short trip, how my life and spirit changed dramatically.

I checked into my hotel and got settled in. I turned on the light switch in the room, then turned it off and then on again... *Ahhh,* I thought to myself, *electricity.* I walked into the bathroom and flushed the toilet. I had to laugh because I actually missed seeing running water. Then I turned on the faucet in the sink and let the water run all over my hands and arms. I lathered up a bar of soap and gleamed with excitement of bubbles. It may seem ridiculous to most but to me it was like heaven. I turned up the A/C and took about a 30-minute shower after that! Room service was ordered and I was back to civilization, finally!!!

It is so true that the littlest things in life can be taken for granted. Years later with all of the treasured memories I hold, I would do that gathering again, in a heartbeat! I am feeling so blessed to be able to look back at the group pic and have the good times come flooding back to me.

CHAPTER 5

THE HUNTER OR THE HUNTED?

After sweet-talking, batting my eyes and lots of blown kisses, I conned my husband into taking me up to the cabin on the snowmobile with instructions to pick me up at 7:30 p.m. after he was finished with chores. With the storms that were now done moving through, it made it too rough for me to risk damaging my Jeep over. Ice and 3-foot snowdrifts were accumulating everywhere from severe wind gusts.

At 3:10 p.m., he called to say he was gassed up and ready. I finished filling my thermos with coffee and headed to the barn. The sky was beautiful and still, finally. With the sun beaming down, the fields looked like diamond mines, glistening and sparkling throughout. Off we were with the one arm around my husband and the other, of course on my Out-back Hat. Couldn't possibly lose that, as we made our way over mounds and around corners to the cabin. We kissed good-bye as he laughed and murmured something about me being crazy and the things I get him into.

It was 3:30 p.m. as I was unlocking the cabin and walking in. It was amazingly warm and sunny in here. I don't think I'll be turning on the heater just yet. Three shirts, Carhardt's and my hat will do just nicely for now.

Set up my chair, load the gun, pour myself and cup of coffee and take out the front window. Now I'm ready, ready to greet what looks like possibly a beautiful sunset followed by a clear star lit night without a cloud in the sky.

My crows noticed I have arrived and just like any other time they stop what they are doing and come fly circles around me and parade with bold harmony their talented flight dancing. They are such great messengers of the woods and fields. If anyone is going to notice movement or danger entering, the crows surely will. Some might take them as just noisy, I look on them as incredible natural guides to the great outdoors. As I close my eyes, I can almost fly with them.

At 4 p.m. like clockwork, I hear the first coyote begin to bark, gathering up the pack. Then another answers back and another. There are many in the area today. Judging by the different tones there must be around 6 of them. The last to bark wasn't very far away and sounds like it's on a chase.

My crows have also heard and are now silent. They will not speak another sound the rest of the night. Once the coyotes start moving, it's the crow's time to head for the pines and roost with the turkeys.

It's been an hour now since I heard the first bark. I have seen nothing move. I've heard only sounds of the pack on a trail of something out here. God's watercolor portrait of another beautiful sunset is almost gone as the first star appears straight out from the window. Darkness is setting in quickly this evening but with the complete snow blanket outside, shapes are easy to identify.

It's now 6 p.m. and time for the heater. I think I'll find my gloves too. It's getting rather brisk outside as the steam rises from my mouth. I'll have another cup of coffee to warm things up and relax.

At 6:15 p.m., something is coming out on the field below running its way up to me. After grabbing my binoculars, I see it's somebody's dog with part of a chain dangling from its collar. Is it hunting a deer or is it being hunted? The coyotes are extremely close now. I can hear their barking echoing through the swamp.

No sooner did those thoughts run through when another object was coming out directly after the dog. It was a coyote. I waited until the dog came up top and took the safety switch off of the gun. With steady hold and watchful aim the dog was passing on through safely but the coyote was gaining ground. As the nose of the coyote came into my scope, I gently squeezed the trigger.

The explosion at the end of the barrel followed with the bright orange flash of fire blinded me for an instant. After regrouping my sight, I noticed that the coyote was hit and down. The dog had gotten its freedom and made its way over the knoll. I looked back at where they first came out in the field and noticed there were 5 more coyotes following the same path. Aiming again hearing the echo throughout the darkness meant, it was a miss. Four turned around and went back into the swamp but one was still determined it was going to have that dog.

Trying to get a good steady aim while my heart was about ready to jump ship, I fired off one more shot. No echo was heard, only that distinctive thud. The second coyote was down.

Silence was falling once again over my fields. Somebody's pet had come out alive. Maybe it will be able to find its way back home to its owner and family. I have never seen that dog in the neighborhood before. It must have been traveling a long way.

The stars are shining bright as I try to replay the entire actions in my mind. One lived and two have passed. But two less coyotes will be rejoining the pack tonight. Two less to attack and devoir savagely our heifers and babies. Two less to kill the deer, turkeys, pheasants and pets.

It's 7:30 p.m. and the snowmobile is on its way. I can hear the remaining coyotes back in the woods trying to regroup and move on to their next victim. I just pray it's not "My" dogs.

Granddaughter Jessica, posing with my double in her pink Carhardts.

CHAPTER 6

VEGAS BABY...
2012 SHOT SHOW

I had recently started my own call company, Crow's Nest Calls. I had heard of the Shot Show over the years working for other companies like Madd/Lohman Game Calls, Circe Calls and Flambeau Outdoors. It was time to take the chance and see what I had been missing. Furthermore, I wanted to see if I could even compete with game call companies that have been out there for years.

After registering with the organization with the proper credentials and such, I booked my hotel reservation and plane ticket. Since I had always frequented Casino's back east here, it turned out that there were several hotels offering me comp on my room, so I chose the one closest to the venue. All I had to do was promise to spend $50 per day at the establishment. Easy I thought and cheap and easy it was!

The Casino was absolutely beautiful AND there was a Starbucks right by the elevator entrance too! There were so many styles of restaurants to choose from daily and buffets too. The stores to shop at right at my convenience was a bit hard to stay away from. I have to admit that I did a lot of window shopping keeping my focus on The Shot Show. The bells and whistles of the slot machines pulled me in quite often but I kept my limit at $50 per day. I did not make it rich in Vegas though! Maybe next time…

The doorman flagged me a taxi and away to the show I went. I had already researched several booths of interest that I felt I should visit. They ranged from first floor, second floor, and third floor and on. Upon getting ready to go inside I was greeted by not one, not two but three Elvis lookalikes! They were a Hoot! I asked for a selfie with them and what a picture it turned out

to be! That pic still turns up in my memories from time to time and I just smile as I remember those men!

OK it was time to suck up my nervousness and walk through those doors. *OH-MY-GAWD!* kept on rolling through my mind. The question of the day was, what have I put myself into? This is what I had set out to do and there was no turning back. Hob Knob with the big wigs sort of thing.

The first floor was packed with booths and people. I was ignored so many times and passed over to even talk or ask about products or intro-duce myself. I had to remind myself that I was a woman in a male dominated arena and

Jessica posing with an Elvis statue in Nashville. She thought Gramma had had to see it! Lol

that I have had to deal with this ever since I crossed that thresh-old of becoming a Predator Hunter. So I thought next will be, floor two and I will only go to those booths that I had book-marked. I no sooner get off the elevator and there was a booth that smiled and acknowledged me. Friendly chaps as they invited me in. They were from a company called NiteSite, which is sadly no longer in business now.

Infrared lighting equipment for on your rifle scope is what they were selling. I had always been against artificial lighting mostly because I hunted by myself and couldn't justify carrying more equipment and juggling with my mouth calls and rifle at the same time. Keep it simple, I always told myself. Since I was a pushover for a British accent coming from them, I was going to give them a chance and see what they had to say.

This concept was like nothing I have ever seen or heard about! To take any daytime scope and attach a few pieces onto your scope and make it visible in total darkness was just blowing my mind. Then they handed me a demo gun stock setup with the equipment and sent me into a blackened hallway. I mean it was totally black. They showed me how to turn it on and right away I saw this target set up all the way down on the wall. Clear as day it was. I could not believe what I was seeing!

My scope that I hunt with has a 50mm lens. It is perfect in half moon to full moon. But on snow covered days, I can get quarter moon to full moon. So there were times that I could not hunt at night because of the darkness to clearly identify my target. I knew right there that I had to have this equipment. The possibilities were endless in my mind. No questions about it! These guys were all great. They asked me about "me". They asked me what brought me here. They made me feel right at home amongst them, which was a total difference from the first floor. We exchanged information and cards that day. I told them I would be in town for three more days. I didn't pull the trigger that day but that equipment was gnawing at me. It was a huge investment for a small company just starting out to justify that price.

The next two days I spent so much time catching up with some of the greats in the industry by visiting at their booths. We spent times talking about doing magazine publications together and how we first met. Talked a lot of hunting together. I finally met one of my old bosses face to face — I just loved working for him and the company for almost 10 years. It was like Old Home Days in Vegas. I needed to be pinched. I really have come a long way. I guess I needed that reality check. I am after all… My Own Worst Critic! Not believing in my worth and value is a lesson I still struggle with. But I am getting better.

The trip home was bit rough. I stilled struggled with that equipment. I was kicking myself not getting it. Replaying in my mind everything they showed me and talked about, the story of how it came about and who developed it was tough to deal with. They even wrote on the card that they gave me, the show price and told me to remind them that I could get it at that price when I was ready. My first thing to do when I got home was talk to my husband about this.

He approved but was skeptical on this equipment. I believe he even mentioned that I was being sold snake oil or something to that effect. So I chewed on it for quite some time.

FAST FORWARD TO 2014

I was invited to The World Predator Wild Hog Expo in Texas. They had asked me to sponsor the "Young Pups Predator Calling Competition" and set me up in a booth with my calls. When it comes to the youth in the outdoors, I am all for it! So, I booked my hotel and flight. It was a scorcher for sure but the event hall was well air conditioned.

I got my booth all set up and a nice display setting around of hides and pics. I handed over the calls from my company for the youth to have and use for the competition. Then I made my rounds to see who else was there. So many old friends were there. It was another Old Home Day for the weekend. Stories, maybe true, maybe not, laughs and good times revisiting the past and hunts were abundant! New friends were also made. Like luck would have it, there was NiteSite. I finally bought a unit and at the show price they offered me in Vegas. I knew after the show I would be doing some hunting out there in Texas and couldn't wait to try it out. But the show was my first priority.

The calling competition was fierce. Some of those adults were not rookies! Some sounds actually gave me chills they were so good! But when the youth hit the stage, my heart melted. There were a couple that I am sure Daddy got them started at a very young age and it wasn't there first rodeo! That didn't stop the younger ones from belting out sounds though! They gave it their best. I couldn't be prouder of all the youth out there showing what they are made of. They got their awards and were very happy to keep the calls as well. I loved when all the kids came back to my stand and wanted me to listen to them calling! That was priceless!

It was time to pack up and wait for my ride to pick me up and head out to my next destination in Texas. I had come with a huge suitcase filled with calls. It was a complete sell out as I left with none. It was a smart thing to put 6 calls away before I even set up. I had some very special ladies that had their names on them.

My ride had arrived as I packed up. They stopped at a restaurant to eat. It was Mexican food. I tried to be polite not wanting them to know that I despise Mexican food so I found something that might be tolerable and ordered that. It was horrible so I did a lot of picking at my plate just to get through the time. I put on a good game face and thanked them for the dinner. Inside I was starving. Every fast food exit just made me hungrier as the miles passed on down the road, all I wanted to do was jump from the car, but I kept it together.

The first thing I did when I got to the next place was charge up my equipment. I was so happy to see a platter of fruit and meats and cheeses setting there waiting for me.

I devoured all I could eat! It was so delicious I couldn't stop. It was like the heavens opened up and the food gods were upon me. Well to me, that was what it felt like but maybe not that dramatic.

After a good night's sleep, we did some hunting. She and the guide were just whispering the entire time at the stand. Pet peeve... no talking or whispering on stand. I knew nothing was going to come in. It was time for me to play with the NiteSite and see what it had to offer. First off, can we talk about the picture! It was so crystal clear and crisp. It was like watching an old black and white, I Love Lucy episode but 100 times better. I could see every detail of the leaves and bark of the trees around me. The equipment took less than a minute to put on. It added 6lbs to the gun that I was using. It might have looked bulky but it was well balanced. You didn't need to look down the scope anymore, just shoulder and shoot which was really cool. This was incredible in every sense of the word! The crosshairs in the screen were the actual crosshairs of the scope. At this point, all I needed was the chatter to stop from behind me and a wild hog or coyote to come out of the brush.

I went to pick the gun off of my shooting stand and all of a sudden, it crashed down. I didn't realize that a piece had vibrated off of the top while it was in the trunk. All of a sudden the attention of the chatty Kathy's were focusing on me now. I was actually reprimanded that, because I was making noise, is why we didn't see anything. I was also reminded that I have to be extremely quiet out there! Whatever, I thought. I'll take the blame and told them I was calling that stand. Ended that night and hit the bed.

Next night the ladies were coming for the evening. I helped get the place cleaned up and organized. We were having a "learn how to call coyotes" demonstration.

OH-MY-GAWD! … don't know what the neighbors thought with all the sounds coming from over the fence, but we had such a great time. I don't remember when the last time I laughed that hard. The food was excellent too! Thank Goodness NO MEXICAN FOOD!

The next day it was back to heading home! I couldn't wait until I got to put my new toy on my own gun and test it out on my coyotes. Out there in the darkness, void of any human chatter or sound, lighting up my fields with infrared, me, in their playground without them knowing… it was such an exhilarating feeling. A song came to my mind as I remembered one of the NiteSite guy's tee-shirt… "Hello Darkness My Old Friend"!

CHAPTER 7

MY SPIRT... MY HOME

Visions can take you on such powerful travels of your mind and soul. You can see clearly, you can feel deeply and you can heal wholeheartedly. In this chapter I will share with you one of the most powerful and beginning visons that I traveled. It was the start of my circle in this life.

Teacher: While working on my book, I was gazing out my back window at the pines swaying to Winds Music. There, not five feet from me, he appeared with only two panes of glass between us. As he stopped in his tracks, he was daring me to look into his eyes and see the message being presented to me by the "GREAT TEACHER".

Face as black as coal, eyes as rich as an ocean blue sky beckoning me to enter as he was branding my soul. Body a bit tattered and old but the face shined with strength, beauty and wisdom. Many nights, I hear him. I hear him call when I visit Mother Tree but never before has he shown himself. I see his footprints imbedded in mud or snow. Wolf has chosen this moment when I need him most. The Great Mystery was calling me to journey.

As the room was filling with the beat of the drums, I allowed my spirit to walk through the cave. It was sometime before I could see light at the end. As I was arriving onto the other side, I was not in my body form any longer. I was coyote and I was traveling and walking my fields. A quick glance to the skies brought my attention to Eagle. Eagle circled above me calling my name and flew into the East. Bear was entering from the north and greeted me as she went about her corn search for her evening meal. Crow was flying into my world and landed on my back.

The animals were full of messages for me. The Coyote was reminding me of being more selective in life's choices. The Bear was my strength and yet was showing the mothering side of things in my family. The Crow was telling me to be aware of life's hints and symbols. The Eagle, which is my East totem, was there to remind me of who I am, what I stand for and where I am headed. And the Wolf, my teacher, was guiding me into the Great Mystery.

Then without warning, I was heading back to the cave entrance. Mountain Lion appeared with one last message for me. He spoke strong and firm of how I must constantly be aware of keeping peace. However, he said, I can never make EVERYONE happy, unless… unless I lie to others or myself. Know it and live it and stop hiding behind masks. Be good to yourself and be true to yourself.

As I was sinking back into the cave and body, my mind was full of new guidance and lessons to ponder. New surges were filling my soul and heart. The drums had stopped. This journey was completing with one remaining question. Where do I go from here with my new messages from the Teacher?

And one answer came down through the winds…

"You already know."

These visons and being surrounded by the animals is one of my life's greatest treasures. To me, it is the biggest college I could ever be a member of. I take great Pride knowing that they have opened their doors to my body, mind and spirit to learn and grow from. They have all taught me Greatest highs, Greatest Lows with a dose of Humility in between. They have taught me Thrills and a sense of danger as well along my Path. One thing for sure is, there are always Lessons to be learned. Which will always bring me to "My Home". Let me share a few of these things to you.

Have you ever listened in the darkness of night to an owl hooting, echoing through the valley? Do you know what it feels like to sit in 20-degree temperatures and breathe in the crisp clean air and feel the tingles throughout your entire body? What about closing your eyes and allowing yourself to sing and dance with the crows in a blustery wind? Or watching shooting stars for hours before the morning sun and wishing on each and every one of them? How about listening and knowing what every footstep on a frosted field belongs to?

And then the sun comes and gently kisses your chilled mountain cheeks with the warmth and paints the sky in pastel colors. The crows come to join you with their jet-black wings sparkling as they turn iridescent. Off in a distance you can hear the turkeys gobbling as they come down from their perch to start their day. Up in the sky the sparrow hawks start circling with brilliant strength and an occasional death-defying swoop to the ground and back up they go once again. The deer are making the journey back to their beds now after feeding and mingling through the night. An occasional stomp to the ground from Momma tells the fawns enough playing now, it's time for bed.

The wind picks up its pace, as you can smell a storm in the air. A symphony plays for you with beautiful and yet chilling notes and keys. The orchestra is the wind. See the branches dance and the blades of grass move to the beat of the music. You can see for miles around you sitting high on top as you watch the first winter snowstorm moving your way. Do you know what it feels like for that first snowflake to land on your nose or catch it on the tip of your tongue and the coolness tickles? The warm tears of happiness gently fall down your cheeks as you can't help but wonder why "YOU" have been blessed with great beauty. How you wish that everyone you know and love could just taste even a little slice of this with you.

I've watched the fawns that could hardly run without falling down, lose their spots and become more independent. I've seen the bucks grow their antlers, shed their velvet and become full-fledged bucks. I've watched the three cubs pounce on Momma Bear in a playful tackle and then Momma in turn, tackle the cubs all the way across the field. I've seen the geese fly North in the spring time and South in the fall. I've watched seasons come and go. I've seen the sun rise and fall and the many phases of the moon.

In the dusk sky if a flat black line streaks through the field, it's a fox. If a little taller line runs and stops, runs and stops, it's a coyote. If I see an upside don "U" slowly move to the other side of the field, it's a deer grazing. The sudden flash before my eyes of wings swooping down to the ground, rustling in the leaves and back up again tells me an owl has found a snack.

People say I never call or write anymore. They say that I'm never home. But I am truly home sitting high on top. My spirit is alive when I am home. My heart beats to a tune of living. My soul dances and drinks the beauty that is before me. So, to all of you who may read this, I offer Nature's Cup and bid you a "Welcome To My Home! Please Do Come In!"

While driving down the road to town on a cool evening. My daughter and I were enjoying the top down on the jeep. Taking in all the sites around us, I started rhyming and started the following lines as she finished it with the perfect ending. Another treasured moment.

THE CROW

By Sheri L Baity and Jamie H Kouba

One Moon

One Star

One Sky

Spread My Wings and Fly

Into the Night We Go

With the Feathers of a Crow

CHAPTER 8

AS THE CROW FLIES ... SO DO I

So many hunts and so many places i have traveled in the past eight years. As the old saying goes: "Time flies when you are having fun!" Not sure if every time was successful or not but i gave it my all. One of my greater moments was when I organized 4 women from Pennsylvania, including myself and 4 women from Texas to hunt hogs and coyotes in Texas. It was a showdown of sorts of the east versus west. With the advice of a good friend, i found a hunting lodge in Victoria, Texas, with plenty of room and bunks to host all 8 of us. I named this hunt "hawgs and dawgs."

I made up gift bags with the logo on them and filled them with my call line and many other things from companies that I have supported over the years. Who doesn't like free stuff, right? With the help of my husband, we strategically loaded up my daughter's vehicle and us East Coasters and hit the road. I thought with 4 licensed drivers, we would get there in good time. Taking turns at driving was also a good plan that worked out well.

We saw so many miles pass on by along our journey. Some were absolutely breath taking but some were not. We made good time getting to Texas. Then at the "Welcome to Texas" sign seemed to drag with accidents and rain. After making it through that mess we were finally closing in on our destination. There were no signs out along the highway saying where this place was so we listened to our GPS and stopped at this gate that said, "You Have Arrived." So I picked up my cell phone and dialed the number for the ranch manager. He said to give him a minute and he would be right up to open the gate. We were all very relieved when we saw him driving up to the Gate, knowing that this was indeed the correct place, wrong gate but right place. We all laughed about this on the drive up to the ranch house.

We unloaded our things and was introduced to our Guide/Camp Master of All Trades, "T" as I will call him. Such a huge Texas welcome came from T. His smile, his handshake and his disposition just warmed you up from head to toe! He couldn't greet us at the gate because he was fixing a delicious welcome meal for us travelers before we head out that evening for our first hog hunt. That man can cook!

Two of the West Coasters had already arrived at camp but we were still awaiting the last two from Texas. We had a great time getting to know the ladies. We talked and laughed already sharing who we were and what we did for a living. I didn't even give it a thought that possibly there would be any personality conflicts amongst us all that would arise, but sadly there was a storm coming. With eight strong women, I should have seen that happening.

The two Texas ladies already picked their beds and myself, my daughter, my granddaughter and my girlfriend picked ours. More talking, snacking and laughing continued in the kitchen as we all watched over a man cooking! It was strange for us in some comical way! Plus, T looked so good doing it! We were like a bunch of Cougars! We should have been disappointed in ourselves but we weren't! It was all in good clean fun!

The last remaining ladies finally hit camp. I could feel a change in the atmosphere almost immediately. As they were carrying their stuff into the ranch house, they immediately started complaining about the beds that were picked. Boss Lady thought that she should have gotten to pick hers before anyone else because she was saying that she was the one that organized this trip with the help of her good friend. Then she called us East Coasters in and said that one of us would have to sleep elsewhere. So, in the good spirit that my girlfriend is, she opted to sleep elsewhere. I felt horrible, but her sweet manner already conceded. That did actually work out beautifully because T gave her, her own private guest bunk house right beside the ranch house. She swore that it was perfect but it wore on me. I thought how rude of Lady Boss.

After a good meal, T started planning out where everyone would sit for the night. Turns out that Lady Boss had pulled aside the ranch manager and told him that this was all her event that she organized and because of that he should be at her disposal, in so many words. So East Coast got T and West Coast got the Ranch Manager. I was very happy to get away from the drama and get in a stand.

Mine was a very cushy two-person ground stand, with windows and a door. Closed in unless you take the windows out. I was only about 30 feet or so from the bait and lights that triggered on when an animal came into the food. Nice comfy seat inside and a steady rest to shoot from. Midnight came with only seeing coons and possums when I heard the side by side heading my way to pick me up. The count that night from the 8 of us was zero. I could still feel the tension when we all got back to camp but quickly dismissed it as I drifted off to sleep.

Morning came to the smell of breakfast and coffee from the kitchen. What a wonderful thing to wake up to. It was delicious!!! My Gawd I just have to adopt this young man and bring him home but I probably couldn't afford him. He did tell me that he was not for sale…lol. Can't blame a girl for trying, right?

After breakfast, I gathered all the ladies around and handed out their gift bags. It was like Christmas. They were thrilled beyond belief. When they asked why, I simply told them that the

Host of this event should give them something to remember this trip. My call line was the icing on the cake. It was demanded that I give a call demonstration and mini seminar. That took up the next couple of hours as we all shared hunting stories as well. For Lady Boss, supposedly organizing this event, had nothing to give out. I felt quietly vindicated. Then I felt bad feeling like that. She did, however soften up her edges just a tad for the remainder of the trip but I was stilled pissed of how she pushed my girlfriend out of the ranch house.

That afternoon, I was the only one suited up to do another hunt from the stand I was in the night before. I took my windows out again and got set up. About an hour had passed when to my left a Momma hog and 8 babies came out on the side by side path. I got into position and tried to steady myself as I put the crosshairs on Momma's head. The wind must have been perfect as she was unaware of me. I squeezed off the trigger. A distinctive thud came and they all scrambled. She headed directly downhill into some of the thickest growth I have ever seen. I knew it was a good hit even though she didn't drop on the spot. So, I called T and told him what happened. He came out to track it but was stopped by the thickness and couldn't go any deeper without equipment. He said it would be best to just get back in that stand tonight. I agreed as we headed back to camp.

Most of the ladies decided that naps would be a good thing to do since we would be staying out later in the night tonight. I decided that an hour power nap sounded good. Again, I woke up to wonderful smells coming from the kitchen along with an occasional singing tune. My first thought as I stirred was I had died and gone to Hawg Heaven! But No, it was T and I was still in Texas!

I decided to eat a little bit more on the lighter side and take lots of snacks and drinks instead. The Ranch Manager picked up the Texas ladies and T took us Pennsylvanian's out to our stands. I am not sure if there were camera's set up at or by my stand but T gave me some very valuable information for my hunt. He had talked about the hog's sense of smell and hearing and how incredible their ability is to detect. He suggested that I keep my door closed and my windows in until I see a hog. Then be quick but quiet as I take the window out and shoot. As soon as the hog lights go on I was to grab my binoculars immediately and look.

About an hour into the hunt the rain started dumping!!! I do mean DUMPING!!!! The only two of us out there was my girlfriend in her closed in ladder stand and me in my closed in ground hut. The other ladies were picked up and taken out of the rainy elements and brought back to camp. About an hour, the hog lights come on as a coyote crosses by the bait. I decided to let him alone and wait for a hog. Two minutes later the lights come back on as a hog stops to eat on the bait. I remember T's instructions as I quietly and quickly took the window out and steadied my gun that was set up with my NiteSite Infrared equipment. It was a perfect black and white movie happening in front of my eyes as I turned it on. I placed the crosshairs on its head and squeezed the trigger. I heard that distinctive thud but this time, the hog went right down. I watched as the tail did a helicopter whirl and then no more movement was seen. I immediately picked up my coyote call and did some coyote vocalizations in hopes that the coyote that had just passed through would come back to investigate. No luck though. I put the window back in and settled back into my seat. I didn't want to call T yet. I just wanted to see if another hog would venture my way.

I have never seen so much rain fall like this. It was as if I was standing under a waterfall or something. Ten minutes had passed since "Hog Down" time and I heard the side by side heading my way. I quickly got my stuff packed up and opened the door with a huge smile on my face. I asked him as he came to the door, "Did you hear the shot?" He was surprised at my question and just passed it off. He said he thought I might want to call it because of this rain and that it was just going to get worse according to radar. He grabbed my gear and gun, then put them in the side by side. He started to drive off and I asked him if he was going to let that hog sit there until morning. He said, "What Hog?" I said laughing, "The one that is just lying there that I shot!!" He looked at me and did a double take as I pointed out the dead hog. He looked back at me as he headed towards the hog and just said, "Well..." He really was a man of few words! Lol

He loaded up the 150 lb. hog in the back. I tried to help but was not very useful. My hands kept on slipping on my grip of the hog but eventually put a two-cent effort in to help finish the job. He said when he left the ranch house that he wasn't expecting to have any hogs to pick up so he didn't load the equipment he would need. I felt bad in my mind of my inability... it was as if I volunteered to go grocery shopping and in the end, he had to push me and the groceries back to the vehicle and load them all by himself. He said don't worry about it, at least I got the hog. That made me feel a little better thinking that Momma was bringing home the bacon.

As we headed off, we made a slight detour to check on my girlfriend and see if she wanted to call her stand and go back to the ranch house. She is one tough cookie as she said she would be staying the night out there. This lady just amazes me every time I think about her. I want to be her when I grow up, is all I can say! So, it was decided that T would swing out in the morning to pick her up.

As we pull in back at the Ranch House, I noticed that the lights were still on. Boss Lady and one of the ladies were still up chatting in the living room. The first thing out of their mouths were, "You can't get any hogs out in this weather!" I walk through the doors, not a stich of fabric on me or my gear is dry. I literally look and feel like I just took a shower with my clothes on.

Although there was a roof over my head in the side by side, there were no doors on it and the wind just kept on blowing the rain in on us. Even my gun got loaded with water as I turned it upside down in the corner and the water just ran out of it. I said with a big smile, "Well, mine is in the back of the side by side." I wish I had a camera to capture the expressions on their faces... it was Priceless!

They handed me a towel. I tried to dry off somewhat as they rushed out to see the hog. Some pics were taken as T told me the weight. He said it was a "good eating" hog. He asked how I wanted it processed. I knew all I wanted was the back straps. So, I decided to have him quarter the rest up. All the ladies from Texas each got a quarter to take home. My girlfriend and I split up the loins.

After a good night's sleep and dry clothing, waking up to food and coffee was a bonus. It was time to settle our affairs and say our good byes. I decided to have the hog head done in a European style mount so I left it there to be done and shipped to me when it was complete. So the score was... Pennsylvania 1 Texas 0.

I was looking for my rifle to pack up as T came walking in carrying it. He had heard about all the water inside of it and took it upon himself to immediately grab it after he processed the hog and clean and oil it up while I slept that night. Then he got up or never slept, I am not sure which and made us coffee and breakfast in the morning. Now do you see why I wanted to adopt him! Last I heard Ladies... He is single!

The trip back home was good until we got closer to Pennsylvania. We were back in snow country which delayed the trip by a day. We chose safety over everything else. It was a good time to reflect and talk about our adventure of hog hunting. I was never happier to see home and share my stories and pics with my husband and fur children. I would go back in a heartbeat if the opportunity would ever present itself.

Me and "T".

Me, my Daughter Jamie and Granddaughter Jessica.

My 165 lb. Hog.

CHAPTER 9

LIKE AN OLD FAMILIAR SONG

Bob Seger and the Silver Bullet Band's song plays in my mind. Telling quite the story of what my life has become over the years. "turn the page" says it all for me.

The miles I have traveled, the people I have met, the hotel/motels that were my home all across the country and the many grounds that I have hunted on are too many to count. What I can say for certain is that I have been blessed with the most incredible family support some people could only imagine or wish for. From the phone calls, sometimes late night to the texts sharing my stories, they put up with it all. They were seeing the change in me that I was unaware of. But never the less, their encouragement and Love kept me turning the page.

My calendar was constantly filling up with seminars at Bass Pro's, Cabela's and Gander Mountain. Before I could catch a breath, various organizations jumped on the band wagon. With a blink of an eye the private hunting camps made their way into my schedules. The personal hunt requests were also added to the list. Some days all I wanted to do was go home to the farm, to my family including my fur children, to my own hunting ground. But a little voice in my head was telling me that I needed to keep on going that I wasn't done yet. So on and on I kept going.

I guess you could say that I was becoming quite the household name in the Hunting Industry. It seemed to fuel up even when I enlisted the help of a Pennsylvania company to develop and produce my own game call line for hunting predators. They turned out beautiful and sounded even better than imagined.

The calls were wooden and with that said, produced the sweetest real to life tones. I had the Whalin Wabbit rabbit distress call, the Casino Crow for crow vocalizations and my all-time go to call was both an open reed/closed reed call for coyotes called the Double Dawg Dare Ya. This company burned my signature into the body of the calls which in turn became the "Signature Line." I was very proud of these calls and decision.

I wanted to have a calling card of sorts. Something more than just a business card was important. I wanted to leave an impact or impression everywhere I stepped my feet on the ground. That didn't take long once people heard my calls and then listened to the animals responding back to me. I have recently closed down the company, Crow's Nest Calls but something inside me is telling me that I am not yet done.

Whalin Wabbit   Casino Crow

Double Dawg Dare Ya

Time will tell. I have become quite comfortable here on my farm and not living out of suitcases anymore. But I do miss, down inside, all the people and places I have crossed paths with. I think about all of the old coyote hunting veterans that I have been blessed to share camp with. I wonder if they ever got to that point and thought about when was the time to retire.

I have been on TV, newspapers, magazines all across the country. There was even a Documentary made about me and my journey. To this day it has not been made public. Hopefully, someday it will be able to be viewed by everyone. That was a humbling experience. Being followed around with camera's and asked numerous questions all day was a new thing for me. But talking about coyotes and hunts was no new thing and I was in my element.

Using the Infrared NiteSite equipment all over the country was always a great thing. Showing ranchers out west that would not allow predator hunting because they were always in fear that someone would shoot one of their animals instead, was so incredible. Once I would power up the unit and they could see with their own eyes the clarity of the animals in black and white. They could identify what species it was from a coyote to a fox to a neighbor's dog to their cattle. All of this was not done for a sale on the equipment, it was done to educate them for future inquiries of hunters that wanted to hunt predators on their property. I wanted them to ask to see their equipment and see if it was safe to use around their livestock. If they didn't come with the right equipment then they were sent away with a "NO!" The bonus always was when those ranchers or farmers would say, "Come on in! Can you take me out and show me how to do this?" And out we would go. Putting a smile and reassurance amongst these hard-working Folks just warmed my heart, over and over again. That was one of the reasons I got into this coyote hunting. I wanted to help my husband who is a dairy farmer and other farmers and ranchers out there that need to protect their livestock against predators. It is too easy for them to become over populated in a pack which in turn causes havoc among livestock.

Being a self-published author was another feather added to my cap. It was called *Coyote Hunting Farm Style*. This was back in 2000, a year before my Dad crossed over. I sure do miss him!

I did two reprints of this and I thought it was all edited. Oh my, the mistakes I found when I saw it in print were horrifying! I even sent it to an old teacher of mine to do the editing for me. He was my favorite high school teacher that I have ever had but I think if I had to grade him he would have to get a "C" on that project.

Now, here I am again bringing the "II" to the table. So, no correcting and sending it back to me…lol. I will try and do better! If you have the first book, you will see that I did add a couple of stories from the first that needed to be in this one.

It has been one crazy ride in over 30 years of coyote hunting. Even though I may grumble at times, I would not change one single thing. I was in the right place at the right time in my life.

Well enough about me. How about if we continue with more memorable stories!…Let us "Turn the Page."

CHAPTER 10

THE CHOPPER SAVED THE DAY

(I know, this chapter title might be a little odd,
but read along and it will become clear.)

It was 5 p.m. As I made my way up to the "Cabin
on the Greens." That's the name I gave my hunting shack
years ago. My dad had named his "Sam's Palace" so I had
to give mine a name too.

I t was a beautiful night with clear skies and moonlight so I wanted to get up there a bit early to see what the deer were up to. The temps were perfect for them with cooler temps. The flies should not be bothering them, so chances are they will be out early this afternoon. There were deer all over so I kept the side by side idled to slow and low speed. I had no runners amongst them so that was a good sign. There were deer out in front of my cabin grazing already so it was one step, two step and slow motion as I snuck to the door and went in. I unloaded my gun and gear and picked up the broom. That is my normal routine every time I get up there. The field mice make a mess while I am not in there. Two of the three mice traps have scored this time. So those old traps get thrown as I put new ones down in their place. I empty my ashtray and start unpacking my gear. Snack and drinks go on my side table, binoculars go on the window sill, then it is on to loading my gun as I put one in the chamber and put it on safe.

I decided to keep my window in and glass through the view. A huge selection of deer were all out. Even the bucks were there as well. There are some nice contenders this year, but that will all depend on deer season and where they are looking for doe at the time. So, I don't get too excited at the moment.

About 125 yards out is a center clump of trees and brush. Three nice bucks are busy scraping and rattling the overhanging tree branches. Then this fantastic buck starts strutting over and the other three bucks run. I don't think those three were in the right place. It is clear that they were trying to lay claim to this guy's territory and he wasn't having it. Quite comical to say the least to watch.

Two hours had passed quickly with this fantastic show out front of my shack. God was starting to pull the shades down on this day and the moon was already up waiting to take over as the nightlight in the sky. I made a wish on the first star as I always do and took out my window. I put my gun in the rest position and start watching and listening. I pulled my binoculars up and start scanning the field. Even though I could still see the deer clearly, I wanted to make sure I could scan the edges of the field and corn field for coyotes. They do have a way of blending in.

My Bushnell Trophy x50 binoculars are perfect for this situation. The 50mm lense has incredible light gathering capabilities. It is almost like daylight and gives great detail to the animals and surroundings. I have always trusted Bushnell to deliver great quality in my binoculars and scopes. They are relatively inexpensive and just as good as those top dollar ones out there in my opinion.

It was 8:17 p.m. and I catch movement coming out of the locust patch. I pick up my binoculars and sure enough, it was a coyote. He was sniffing around and mousing towards the corn patch. I took my gun off of safe. I fired up my infrared and got him in my site, waiting for him to stop before he was covered by the corn was nerve wracking.

So, I blew him the kiss of death. A sudden stop gave me the opportunity to take the shot as I slowly squeezed off the trigger. He dropped then got back up and ran into the corn. Dang I had a feeling that I would not be finding him that night.

As I packed up my stuff and decided to head back home, I took a drive down there to the point of impact. There was definitely a blood trail headed straight into the corn. I drove around the corn field just a bit to see if it came out the bottom but saw no signs of it. Back home it would be as I made my way.

I told my husband about it the next morning, He was right into chopping the corn to fill the silo. He just got a new to him, used chopper from Larry Romance & Son Inc. out of Woodhull, NY. His old one was getting ready to, as my husband put it, blow apart. We dealt with a great group of guys over there. Larry and Kyle were so knowledgeable and not pushy at all. We settled on a New Holland P.T. Forage Harvester Model FP230.

After telling my husband the story, he said, "Great! That's the field I'm heading to this morning!"

That corn over back is about 12-14 feet tall. The ground is uneven for me to try and get through it, so I thought this was the perfect way to find a coyote that just might be laying there.

After feeding breakfast to my pups, I decided to head up to my cabin and watch him chop. He made the first round with no stops. My gut was not comfortable as I wondered if I wounded one and it got away. That does not sit well with me. The second round was the same thing with no stop.

He started the third round and I saw him stop and then back it up a bit. He got off his tractor and I saw him walk into the corn a bit, bend down and pick up the coyote from last night. He held it up in the air towards the cabin to show me! I immediately came down with the side by side and loaded it in. It was a 34 lb. female. It had no signs of nursing so this was definitely not a Momma.

So, the search had ended perfectly. I owe a great bit of thanks to Larry Romance & Son, Inc. And a big howdy to Larry and Kyle that made the deal of a newer to us chopper that performed perfectly! Who knew that a chopper would save the leg work!

CHAPTER 11

TWO FOR THE MONEY

I had an opportunity to take a veteran out for a DMAP doe tag. We had a lot of does that needed thinned out desperately. Corn and alfalfa were being eaten up like crazy. There is an acceptable point of eating and then there is a point where they're eating too much and we end up with not enough to fill our silo for our cows. Unfortunately, this was the critical point that was approaching us.

I had a game warden hunting here and he couldn't believe the excessive amount of deer on our property. That is when he suggested to us to get enrolled in the DMAP program where they issue doe tags for anyone wanting to thin down the herd. I had a lot of hunters that took the chance at a doe but out of 25 tags issued, no one was successful.

My veteran was the last to try his luck. Something told me to put him down in the old cow pond next to the lilac bushes. Since he was well educated on hunting and safety, I decided to head to my shack and settle in for some possible coyote hunting. I was looking for a coyote that I had named "Mr. Chocolate" due to the incredible rich brown tones he had throughout his fur. He was also quite huge in size. I couldn't wait to get him on a scale.

The deer were hardly moving because of the heat and time was ticking away towards ending deer hunting for the evening. I got inside my shack and got all set up as I took my window out. Loaded up my gun and got it in the rest. I wouldn't need my infrared equipment on my gun because we would be done at dark and head back to the house.

The lilac bush was a hot spot right before dark, so I knew he would have an excellent chance. I had high hopes for him. Unless you are moving around, there should be no reason why you didn't see anything.

The crows were still chatting and flying around. I had heard no shots from the veteran so I just took "Nature's Cup" all in for all it was worth. There truly is healing in this special place of mine. I could get lost in time and sometimes I really do. From the smells, the feathered one's flights, to the tree's dancing in the wind, it draws my soul in completely.

I decided to not do any coyote calling that evening. I didn't want to mess his deer hunt up, so I just sat and waited. I have been seeing Mr. Chocolate every time I have been up here in the evening about a half hour before dark. I thought tonight might be the night to put a stop to him.

It was 6:40 p.m. as I saw movement to my right. I was already hunched down scanning the fields as I slowly grab my gun and get it into position. I have the lead one in my scope. I squeezed off the trigger and the first one dropped. As I went to chamber another round, the casing got stuck. I shook the gun and it rolled out. I chambered another round and to my surprise the second coyote was still standing still there and looking around. I got the coyote into my crosshairs and fired off the second shot and down it went.

Rather than going to get them, I decided I should wait until my veteran was done hunting so I just kicked back and enjoyed the gorgeous sunset. About another 20 minutes had passed and my Veteran was knocking at my shack door. He had asked me if I missed. I told him no but we had to go get them. He was shocked to hear it was two and not just one. It was tracking time!

I started up the side by side and headed out into the field. It was dark by now so finding them would be a bit difficult. The hay was so high. We both had flashlights. I sent him walking in one direction and I headed in the opposite way. Within about 5 minutes of searching, I hollered to him that I found one. I started dragging it back to the side by side. It wasn't two minutes later and he was hollering that he found the other one. I told him to wait right

there and I would be over to get him and the coyote. I loaded up mine and went to him. We loaded up the other coyote and headed back to the farm.

We were both chatty Kathy's on the ride back to the farmhouse. It was so exciting to be able to share that with someone. I didn't even think to weigh these two but they were both almost identical males from size to markings to coloring. I would bet they came from the same litter. Either way, two less to cause destruction on my wildlife up back. I am sure that the deer had a good night after that up there.

I have shared these hunts with many people but to actually host a veteran, and to let him experience the outdoors on a private farm felt even better.

They have given so much for me to be able to do what I do. Their guts, their drive to serve and protect and their passion to give it their all gives me every ounce of respect for them. They are amazing young men and women! I thank them all and salute them!!!

So, if you have never taken a veteran out to experience the outdoors, I highly recommend it. To watch them out there, to see in their eyes what they are experiencing and seeing is incredible. I guarantee you will thank yourself for it!

CHAPTER 12

MY SECOND FAMILY

It all started 19 years ago when Laporte Fire Company out of Sullivan County needed a speaker on coyote hunting for their annual coyote hunting contest. There were other fire companies involved in this annual contest as well. They found me somehow and asked if I would do it. Well, since my father was a member of three fire companies in the past, I felt it was a way to honor him in some way for all of his years of service. I of course jumped at the offer and made my way over.

Actually, I made my way over at the start of the hunt. The firemen wanted to learn how to coyote hunt also. I met up with several guys including Dan "The Man" and Mikey, that night as we prepared to go out hunting. Dan

and Mikey would be the first two "Brothers" that adopted me into the fold.

Dan "The Man" is a sassy young whipper snapper as I affectionately choose to call him and Mikey is an adorable, sweet, loving Teddy Bear that has this laugh that is infectious in the best way possible. We have the true Brother and Sister relationship that any family could possibly have. We pick on each other, we sass to no limit. I always threaten to tell Dan's Mom on him and he just says, "Go

My Firefighter Brothers from LaPorte and surrounding areas.

Ahead" as he has that mean look on his face and laughs at me. But once in a while Mikey and I can put on our best poker faces and get one over on that young whipper snapper and it feels so good!!!

There has got to be a school somewhere out there that I can take a

course on how to be more successful at my attempts. I will keep on searching. Truth be told. I would be lost without those two in my life and all the rest of the Fire and Emergency guys and gals. But don't tell Dan The Man I said that. His head will swell and it won't fit in his Chief's helmet! Even after 19 years I still find myself going back for more torture from Dan. As God is my witness, I wouldn't have it any other way. I not only live for another year to possibly get one over on him plus, he is my Brother to me in my heart and soul and that is Priceless!

Dan is married to a Saint of a woman who can put up with his nonsense and reign him in when needed. I have no idea how she does it. She is like the Whipper Snapper Whisperer or something! She is my Idol! One could learn from her for sure!

Then there is their son. It has been surprisingly wonderful watching this kid grow up to this young man. He has a playful smile about him that just makes everything ok in this world. I can't wait to see where life takes him. We ladies must keep his time with his Dad limited… lol. That kid is also a phenomenal hunter!

Dan's Mom and Step Dad are also Great People. The work they have put into that Fire Station, beyond the 19 years I have known them, is incredible, selfless, courageous and a Beautiful Staple for the community. I have asked them several times to adopt me but I'm thinking that Dan veto's the matter! I think the world of them both and send sympathies for having to deal with Dan too!

Then there is Mikey, also a Veteran, Thank You for your Service. I remember one thing about my Dad, he could wrap you up in his arms so tight and you would just melt and know that everything will be ok, no matter what. You can ask anyone what they miss about him and they would all say it's his hugs. That would be Mikey. I Love those hugs every chance I get. It's like getting a hug from my Dad from heaven. Mikey has that same touch.

While taking care of his folks and running a bar, he still makes time to serve his community in Fire and Rescue. With courage and mindset, he is one amazing individual. I am just waiting to hear that he has found the "One" in his life. He deserves all the happiness that life can give him!

Then there are countless others that I have not mentioned by name. Most of them were kids just starting out in the departments and learning the ropes of Firefighters. They have all blessed me and made me feel right at home. I truly "Thank" them for this. Now all of these years later, they have grown up and are raising their own families and still dedicating themselves to this community.

Year after year, it is a flip a coin kind of situation. You never know what you will or won't get. Before Dan chimes in, I will own that there will also be a miss during these hunts. Yes, I missed! That kid will never let me forget it so I might as well admit it here in print! Lol In the dark hours of hunting and lack of sleep, there are lots of laughs, rushing moments, coyotes talking up a storm and ending the contest with nothing to show for our efforts. But we keep on coming back to do it again next year.

I thought I was done last year, it was a bad start with a broken rib. I managed to get myself through the hunting aspect but come weigh in day, I was a hurting pup. My seminar sucked. I couldn't even think about the words or subjects I wanted to touch on, my documentary was not loading and the pain was killing me. All I could focus on was the pain.

So, after it was over I apologized to Dan and Mikey for the crappy seminar and then told them that this was my last time. I told them I just can't do it anymore. They saw it coming and said they understood. But guess what... after taking a long time to heal and get my head back in the game... I am coming back for 20 years of my part to help support the Fire Companies of

Sullivan County! Maybe we will actually get a coyote to weigh in. I am bound and determined to get our names on that list!

The last day of the hunt at the Fire Station is always hopping. Final weigh-ins and a seminar from me as the chairs start to fill in. The station puts on a feast for all that entered in the hunt.

So many selections of food, from salads to chili, to desserts and drinks. I get exhausted just thinking about all the work that went into these choices. I am getting hungry just now thinking about it.

So many people I have met. I've exchanged stories with so many hunters. I got to see the dog hunters, the electronic callers, and the mouth callers too. So much knowledge packed into one weekend of the year.

The people that I have met, the friends that I have made and the ones that come back to listen to what I have to say are priceless! Each year I am blessed with someone or something new. One year after my seminar as I was packing up, this beautiful older couple came in carrying a wooden crow. It read "The Crows Nest" and "75" on the wing. It is a little over 3 feet long. It was on their house when they moved into the community.

They didn't know what they were going to do with it until they came and heard me speak. Once they saw my companies name was Crow's Nest Calls, the wife sent her husband over to their house and retrieve their crow sign. He came in and they presented it to me. I must admit a few tears fell. They told me the story of how it came about and said they knew right away where it needed to go. It is currently in my office, hanging in front of my computer. Every time I sit down at my computer, my eyes first go to the crow and I smile inside and out! I don't think they realize just what this has meant to me.

Then we have Wendy and Penny, who are twins. We mostly talk anything coyotes and hunting. Beautiful ladies all the way through. I have added them on my Facebook account. I get to see what is happening in their life. I love seeing their hunting adventures, their family travels and watching their children and grandchildren as they grow. My heart went out to them as the news hit that their momma with Alzheimer's had finally crossed over. They still reflect on her from time to time in their posts. There are not enough words in the dictionary that can describe these two sisters. I am in awe of their strength!

There is also the year that two young kids made a documentary on me and the hunt contest which is still not made public yet. These boys were so smart and brilliant on the film they laid down. Incredible talent and beautiful personalities.

They were so thirsty for learning all aspects of what goes into coyote hunting, the why's of a contest, the biology behind the samples that were being taken from the coyotes by the students at weigh in's. Will and Luke are their names. I Love them as if they were my own sons. Their Momma's certainly raised them right. It was hard being mic'd and followed around with a camera for four days. But what they put together was incredible. Will was doing this for his thesis in his master's program. I

Will, me and Luke — my Documentary guys.

am proud to have been good enough to be a part of it! I am so very proud of them both!

I don't think they realized just what they were getting themselves into until the first night of a coyote hunt. They froze their behinds off the entire weekend. Lots of hand warmers, boot warmers, blankets and whatever else we could find to keep them in the game. Lol But they were determined to keep following us and to not miss a bit of filming opportunities. In all fairness, I will say that the weather that weekend was brutal and relentless! Frigid temps and the winds that blew through with furry made the temps just plain nasty.

I have been around many hunters that have asked questions in the last 30-plus years but these two young men just blew my mind. And every time I gave them a response, it was like the lights went on in their head. Many of those questions they asked over the 4 days, I have never been asked or would have never thought to be asked. It is very clear to me that they have a great and bright future in the filming industry! I wish them both a very prosperous future in the filming industry!

I can't forget mentioning my very own concierge, bartender, cook, waiter and friend Bob Bob. I don't think that man even owns a frown. Always happy to see me every year. No matter which bar he is working in at the time, I make sure to stop on by. He greets me with a big ole smile and hug. I feel like royalty the minute I walk through the door. I always hope that he is still doing his job year after year. It will be a very sad day when he retires!!! Thank You Bob Bob for being my friend.

With all the good in these contests you also have to expect the bad to sprinkle down on your parade. The occasional death threats were there from time to time. Luckily, I remembered something that a dear old wise seasoned coyote hunter told me. He said, "You know you've become famous in the arena when you get your first death threat!" He was right, my name had certainly become frequently talked about. This in turn made me and the Fire Stations the target for the anti-hunter groups across this Country.

One year there was threat of a protest, but never happened. The next year, they sent a reporter in pretending to write about the hunts success and the hunters that participated in it. Then within a month the articles came out with so many lies and twisted information, it was just disgusting and ugly. Then they had the audacity to use my name and said these were my words and quotes, which were never what I would ever say. So, it was easy for me to find the source.

I finally sent them a Cease and Desist order to their doors and gave them a timeline of one week to pull all articles off of all social media that had my name in it. They never got my permission to use my name and they never spoke to me at all. It only took one day after they did this before everything was erased. Don't be messing with The Crow... I will circle around and crap on your head!

And last but not least there are the Cliques that I had to deal with. You know the types, the ones that are seeing someone else, mostly a girl, getting more attention than they are regarding coyote hunting in the media and talk amongst thousands of hunters. Let's just say they were all eventually blocked from my social media. This was sad, because I had a lot of respect for those hunters. In my opinion we were all of equal quality in our hunting abilities but because I was a woman, the media grabbed that angle and ran with it. To some extent it was extreme and aggressive and apparently a hot new topic of discussion. I had no control over the attention.

At a time of the Bill making, I valued and respected a joining of forces to support this great endeavor with hunters across Pennsylvania. That was the Bill HB1188 that I got a State Rep to write up. The next 3 ½ years were spent on traveling this state, regardless of what these cliques were trying to insinuate, with my own money, time, and miles to educate the Game Commission, various Organizations, Senators, State Reps and the Public. One thing my Dad always taught me was to, no matter what, stand in your truth! I will live in those words until the day I take my last breath! Thank You, Daddy!

Finally after going through the House Reps and then Senate, it was handed over to the Governor to sign. Then it was back to the Game Commissioners to plead my case to change the law for Predator Hunters across Pennsylvania to allow Infrared and Thermal to be used for Predator Hunting. What a celebration that was!!! I will always look at 2020 as the year that "Good" came about for all of us Hunters!

Then 2024 came along with being back at the Coyote Hunt with Laporte. This time no broken ribs, I put on another great seminar for a packed fire house. No coyotes were taken with me and the guys, once again. The coyotes were extremely vocal as always. Great laughs and memories were added to the 20 plus years with this Family!

Here I sit... 2025 is soon approaching and I can't wait to be among my brothers and sisters once again in Sullivan County. Watch out Dan... your sister is coming back and bringing her "A" game! Lol

I don't know how many more years I have left but I can say for certain that year after year I will forever treasure spending time with "My Family" of Laporte and the surrounding area. You very rarely meet genuine people in today's world. But when you do... take it all in and Thank God for his blessings!

CHAPTER 13

THE MAN BEHIND MY DRIVE

I will be the first to admit as I got into my teen years, I put my dad through hell.

Samuel M. Barnes 12/12/34–04/04/01.

Up until then, I was Daddy's Lil Girl. Then the next hundred years, ok, maybe not a hundred... lol, my mind just couldn't stop being a gypsy, from one man to another, from one city to another from one thought to another, I was not clear on what I thought was right for me and my daughter. Some days now, as I look back, I wonder how my daughter can still look up to me, if I'm being honest! I also wonder how my Dad got through those years too. Maybe that's why he was bald and grey. Through all of that, he was always there, not letting me fall and always encouraging me.

Maybe... just maybe, he should have let me fall... just once to knock some sense into me. He thought more of me than I ever thought of myself. Whenever I would go to leave it was always the biggest hug ever that made me think that everything would be OK. Every phone call ended with an "I Love You!" I wondered so many times how he could still show and give so much to this broken child. What could he possibly see that I didn't?

As I started coming to my senses and growing up finally, I just had one mission... I wanted to make my Dad proud of me. I wanted to get my life together for my daughter and my Dad. I eventually did but I was still in thought that getting myself together was not all I could do. My Brother and Sister had great lives. Very successful in deed. But there was always me just getting by.

I think me getting into hunting and marrying a dairy farmer was a step in the right direction. Before I knew it, he was coming up hunting all the time and we were building shooting shacks with my husband. We then expanded and built ourselves cabins, complete with beds, pull out windows and propane heaters which were upgraded later to wood stoves. Thanks to my husband, we got Boujee so to speak...lol

My coyote hunting started to become famous in the media and picking up steam. Phone calls from men wanting to know my secrets. Then the newspapers started doing interviews. The magazine stories followed along with TV shows. It was crazy. I was somewhat private in my life but I thought if I wrote a book and got it out there that I could go back in my hermit stage side of me. But that was not good planning on my part and it came in like a landslide. The media loved to use tag lines like Woman Coyote Hunter or Woman Coyote Slayer.

Through all this time I still wondered if my Dad was proud of me, yet? He would never say anything so I kept on going to just hear him say it once. That was all I thought I needed. I was still getting the hugs and the I Love Yous but I felt like there was something missing. I got hired on at MADD and Lohman game calls and started traveling and doing seminars. I called him after every event and every hunt to tell him all about it.

One day he asked me if I would take him coyote hunting. I was thrilled. We got up there about an hour before dark to my "Cabin on the Greens." By this time in life I had pretty much instilled the habit of moving in slow motion, not making loud noises or talking out loud. I was very regimented in my hunting routine and proud of it.

It was about 10 minutes before dark on a moon lit night. Looking through my 50mm binoculars and scope was like daylight. I was slowly glassing the field when I started hearing his chair squeak. I looked over and saw him quickly get up and then wrestle his snack bag and find a treat. Then the loud pop of a soda can rang out in the silence. Then he asked in a normal loud voice if I wanted anything. I quietly whispered No, hoping he would get the message to not make noise. But that didn't work and I went back to looking for coyotes. Then loud footsteps of heavy boots as he walked back to his shooting seat along with the squeaky chair were like sounding an alarm to anything that might have thought to think twice before showing their face!! Lol

So, I leaned out of the window view and whispered to him… "Shhhhhh, Dad, you can't make a bunch of noise. You will scare the coyotes away!!!"

It was then that a huge grin came to my face. My memory bank opened up like a flash of lightening. It was when I was about 7 and we were fishing a small stream trout creek. Correction, he was fishing and I was skipping rocks. I couldn't wait to get back home and tell my brother that I finally learned how to skip rocks. I remember it clearly like it was yesterday! My Dad leaned over to me and whispered… "Shhhhhh… You can't skip rocks. It will scare the fish away!!!" They say you become your parents at some time in your life. That was that moment.

When he passed away in 2001, his funeral was huge. He belonged and volunteered at 3 fire companies. Many other companies knew of my Dad as well. They brought the ladder trucks at the front of the funeral home and hoisted the American Flag across the roadway. The Fire companies even flew their flags at half mass. One by one the men and women came through the line and offered condolences to us all. They had the black band over their badges. Some wore sunglasses to hide their tears running down. Almost every single fire rescuer told me that, my Dad was so proud of me and

he talked about me to anyone that would listen. I never knew that. All this time I was feeling that I was still a failure.

I don't know but maybe because he lost his Dad at 14 and he didn't hear it as a child either. He always thought and said repeatedly that he was the worst Father to us. To me he was the Best! I wish everyone had a Father figure like him.

Looking back, I see how much he Loved his community including all the neighbor kids, the political letter writing campaigns he did to get assistance for the fire companies, giving his shirt off his back to whoever needed it and to loving and trying to instill guidance for this broken child. I can knowingly say that I am proud of him as I now know he is proud of me! Thank You Dad for not giving up... You did good kid, as he used to say!

CHAPTER 14

THE FACE-OFF

I hadn't been up to my "cabin on the greens" in quite a while. Deer season was just around the corner. I was curious what the bucks that might be wandering around the farm looked like. It was going to be clear skies with no wind and almost a full moon. I decided it would be a beautiful and relaxing night to head on up.

I t was almost dark. The fields were loaded with deer already. I geared down on the side by side and slowly made my way as close as I could get without scaring the deer. I counted 27 as I slinked my way into my cabin. I unpacked my gear and got my gun loaded because... you never know. Got my binoculars out and started glassing. The does mostly stayed past the dip but all the bucks were about 30 to 50 yards straight out from me. I immediately thought, "You know it is not deer season because this show would never happen…lol!"

The woods were painted with gorgeous fall colors. Soon God's watercolors will paint the sky above. What a spectacular show that will be, I thought to myself. Just when I thought that it couldn't get any better a Bald Eagle glided across my front window. The beauty and the grace as those huge wings effortlessly went across the sky was magnificent! My heart skipped a beat for sure!!!

The turkeys must have thought it was their time to head to the roost for the night. As they waddled their way across the field. This year's fawns were curious and thought it was a good idea to investigate. The turkeys put them in their place really quick. It was a comedy show for a few minutes. I had to chuckle at the innocence of the fawns. They were back to their Momma's in no time at all.

I sunk in to every quiet, peaceful moment I could capture. There is always something magical about this place. It rejuvenates my entire body, mind and spirit. Very rarely do I go up there and not see or hear anything. Having a bad day, go to the cabin. Feeling grumpy, go to the cabin. Feeling sad, go to the cabin. It is without a doubt, my healing spot.

A few minutes later it was like an Alfred Hitchcock scene when the crows decided it was their time to head to the pines for the night. Hundreds of them flew over me. Some did their wing dances and cawed out. I cawed back to them. My heart fluttered with joy. I love how they know I am no threat to them. I also appreciate how they don't tell the other animals that I am here.

God was starting to pull the shades down on the sun as the colors started to illuminate the night canvas. Yellows, pink, blue and gold just beautifully blended in his artwork. Breathtaking does not even describe this piece of art. Many of artist could try to recreate this but I have doubt that anyone could succeed.

The bark of the first coyote was heard. It didn't seem to affect my herd of deer that was still grazing out in front of me. The does picked their heads up but went right back to eating. About 30 seconds after that the rest of the pack answered back with one bark. Then the chorus sang out with yips and howls. I love to hear that — Natures Symphony at its best.

So many people get chills hearing this, but I am the odd duck. I am like... give me more!!! The sounds that come out of their choir is incredible! The more I hear them, the more that I want to be a part of them and learn to sound just like them. I try and sometimes I can get a few notes correct, but not always. But at least I do try and fit in when they light up. They don't stop while I am singing too so I must be doing an OK job!

An hour had passed by since the coyote's roll call. The deer were still calm, some to the point of laying down. The moon was lighting up the fields. I powered up my NiteSite and turned the Infrared down a bit. I didn't need that much with the moon beams. I stretched my scope a bit more to the far left of my window and saw a coyote mousing its way towards the bucks. Mr. Big Bucks seemed to spot it at the same time I did. Unfortunately, I could not take a safe shot because of the deer behind it on the horizon of the field so I patiently waited. The coyote was more interested in mousing and didn't even realize that the deer were there.

Finally, the coyote got its nose off the ground and was practically face to face with Mr. Big Bucks. Just like that... we had the Face-Off. It was like they were both waiting for the coin toss by the referee to see who went first. The other bucks were slowly moving away from the danger. At last, I had a clear shot free of other deer in the scope. The buck stomped but still stood firm. The coyote started gearing up for the lunge with his body movement... then...

The shot rang out in the darkness. My .243 did its job well. That distinctive thud of an impact shot was heard. The coyote spun and dropped almost immediately! Mr. Big Bucks never moved. He just stood there and stared. Then he snorted and went back to eating. The does had run for the stone wall but still stayed way out to the edge of the fields. Most of the other bucks joined them but the bigger bucks stuck around with the big guy.

I decided to let the coyote lay until the next morning. I didn't want to disrupt the deer and I knew right where he dropped. I sat around enjoying the scenery, stars and even a few shooting stars were gracing the sky. The deer that ran towards the woods eventually settled back down in the fields. I ended up staying for another two hours until all the deer headed for the corn field down below. I figured it was safe then to load up and head off the hill in the side by side without scaring them.

Morning came as I finished my first cup of coffee and headed up on the hill. I watched a Bald Eagle circling over that field where the coyote was. I went on out and checked to see if the bullet went straight through, which it did. Before I leave a meal for the winged ones, I like to make sure there is no bullet left inside to hurt them in any way. Just something I have always thought about and done.

He had good sharp teeth. A little on the small size but hefty in muscle tone with big paws. I think if he would have survived he would have grown up to be a big boy. If I had to guess, I figured he was about 30 pounds in weight. He already was filling in a nice winter fur.

Since the Eagle was watching me from the treetop, I snapped a quick picture of this young male and let him lie. I made the decision to let the Eagle have a good meal. It is a pleasure for me to feed my winged ones from time to time. I am sure the ravens, crows and hawks will feast as well. I checked back a week later and there was nothing left to pick out of the hay field except for the skull. I dropped that off at the old foundation on my way back to the farmhouse where more coffee awaited me.

All in all, I saw some good contenders for deer season and I was able to take out one more threat for our wildlife, our cows and our beefers on the farm.

Another successful hunt for the books.

CHAPTER 15

PEOPLE ASK ME... WHY THE CROWS?

I have always loved crows. Their beauty in the sunlight, wing dances and their vocalizations are mesmerizing. Until I started hunting, I didn't know how valuable watching them would become and that it would be such an important tool in my toolbox.

Many years ago I was gifted with the name of Crow Woman (Koga-a-ge-ha). I had taken a dead crow to my friend John and asked to restore its beauty so that it could live again. I was devastated that a neighbor had shot and killed it because he said it was harassing a hawk. Anyone in their right mind knows that the hawks harass the crows, not the other way around. The hawks are famous for raiding the crow's nest to either get the eggs, the babies or kill a crow.

A week later John called me and asked to come see him. When I got there, he presented me with the skull all cleaned, the feet and the hide beautifully preserved and dried flat. He had the tail and wings spread as if it was ready to take flight, once again. That is when I was gifted with my name.

Before I left he said to me, "This is your name going forward. Because of you, Crow will live. Because of You, Crow will Fly once again. Crows Beauty will always be within you!" Those powerful words will stick to me until the day I take my last breath. John has since passed away but I hope he can see how I carry on his message to this day.

I started watching and listening to my crows every time I was out in the outdoors. Watching their movements, listening to their vocalizations, their interactions with the other wildlife and the sentinels. I learned by all of this that I able to know what danger was coming through the woods and where it was going to come out at. I watched the other animals also pay attention to the crow's messages. That is also when I realized the importance of having a crow call with me when hunting predators.

With a crow call, I have learned that I can portray that I am a crow or call the crows and with that I can peek the predator's interest. The reason for this is that coyotes always want to know what the crows are eating on. While peeking their interest I have a pretty good chance at a shot.

This is why I always blow the crow call along with coyote vocalizations.

Here in Pennsylvania my success has been few and far between with a rabbit distress, no matter where in the state I use it. Now out west the rabbit call won far more times than not. But being loyal to what the crows taught me, I would still add the crow call to the scenario.

So, there you have it. The answer to your question... Why the Crow?... And the story behind it. Fly Crow Fly!!!

CHAPTER 16

TIPS, TACTICS AND A BAG OF TRICKS

Let's start with the basic gear I have chosen to go with for over 30 years. Keep in mind that these are only my choices that have worked for me. As I have said at many seminars, "Find what works for you!!!" I could not be any clearer about this.

GUNS

My second year of hunting, my husband bought me a, new to me, Winchester Model 70 .243. Beautiful wood stock and well balanced to shoulder up. That was the start of my success of many hunting stories to come. Her name is Stella. This was not a bush gun which was fine with me. I Love that it is a flat shooting gun. So, for fields and open woods it can reach out there and touch the target.

It has gone through many changes over the years and even put in retirement no thanks to a couple of "gunsmiths" that apparently didn't know squat. But now Thanks to the amazing Jeremy of The Gun Fix, out of Benton PA, she is all properly fixed, sighted in and ready to come back out of retirement. I am so excited to create new memories with her again.

While Stella was not usable, I purchased a Savage AXIS .243. I named her Stella 2.0 because she is black in color, sexy and smooth shooting with a perfect weight for me to carry and shoulder up. Together we carried on with making memories. I will be putting her on a leave of absence while Stella joins the world of hunting once again for a while but also feel comfortable knowing that I always have a backup waiting at home if the need shall arise.

I Love the .243's. I call them my every gun. Whether it be groundhogs, predators, deer or even bear, with the proper shot placement, it will go down. Don't get me wrong, I am human and there is that occasional swing and miss shot that happens from time to time and **I will own it**. I call it Operator Error... lol.

AMMUNITION

For ammunition, I have always used Winchester Power Point in a 100 gr. I have not had one bad bullet in all the boxes that I have gone through in 30 years. And as far as the taxidermists go, they haven't complained about the entrance and exit holes either. The exit holes have measured about a quarter inch in size.

SCOPES

When I started out I had used Tasco Golden Antler with a 50mm objective. As far as the scopes go that both of my guns now have are the Bushnell Banner 6x18x50. The light gathering capability of this beauty is incredible with the 50mm!!! With a half-moon to full moon, it is like shooting in near to close daylight. Snow cover I can see clearly from quarter-moon to full moon without using artificial lighting of any sorts. Since I have mostly hunted by myself starting out, I looked for something that would be less equipment I had to carry around and fumble in the dark.

INFRA-RED OPTICS

About 8 or 9 years ago I discovered Infrared equipment through a company called NiteSite. Very sadly though through mismanagement at the upper level, they are no longer in business. As luck would have it, I still have my unit and back-up units to use. I sure do miss those guys in the Texas office! So many memories of the travels together to the Harris-

NiteSite Crew. Back Row, L-R, Steve, Marty and Peter.

burg Show and chatting on the many phone calls. They got right on board with me when I started the bill to allow Infrared and Thermal for predator hunters in Pennsylvania. In July of 2020 they closed the doors. In October of 2020 the law was changed to allow the use of this equipment. They just could not hold on any longer for all the potential future sales in this state. I can say that Steve and Marty will always be considered as "My Brothers From Another Mother!!!"

Thank You Guys for the wonderful journey together and your support! I will be forever grateful...

BINOCULARS

Now onto Binoculars we go. When choosing strength I shop for the same mm objective that I use in my scope and simply because of the light gathering capability, so I use Bushnell Trophy x50. So again, the same outcome is true with my scope, light gathering without artificial lighting. They are crisp and clear with great comfort and fit for long glassing periods.

While choosing all of these types of products and coming to use the Bushnell products, one thing that is also true is affordability! I am not a rich person and hunting can get really expensive. Sometimes before you know it, the bank card is hollering at you and your spouse is saying... WHOA!!!!! I am not sponsored by Bushnell products at all! I just want people to know that there are products and companies out there that in my opinion have the same quality at affordable prices that won't break the bank.

RANGEFINDERS

Rangefinders are the last of my gear. I bet you can guess right now who I chose to use…lol. I chose the Bushnell Legend Rangefinder. Simply put, ease of use, clear, accurate and affordable! Doesn't take up much space at all in my bag of tricks. It slides right into my backpack outer sleeve for easy access. It fits my hand well which is nice to not have excessive bulk. The buttons are practically feather light to push and get readings. I Love Bushnell… yet another trusted product of theirs that I carry and use often.

CAMOUFLAGE

I will only do a very short paragraph or two on camouflage only because i have yet to be satisfied on warmth for long sits or non-bulk!

I have tried men's brands to women's lines to layers of different textures from low costs up to high end costs and have still not found my company that I can get behind. You should have seen all the different camo that I donated to the local thrift store last year. I am talking about 55-gallon trash bags of stuff! That is not even talking about all the stuff I have given away. I do love anything real tree as far as concealment for my areas that I hunt, but that is all I have going for me.

I do remember when I first started out I came across these silk long johns online. They were the softest and warmest thing I have ever had! Unfortunately, within a few years, they had started to snag and sadly had to hit the can. I have yet to find them online again to this day. I had a wonderful friend in the coyote hunting business. When I was starting out, he told me secretly that he wore women's pantyhose for warmth. He swore by them! I haven't tried that idea yet, who knows, maybe this will be the year! Do they even make pantyhose anymore? Oh, he was a pistol — full of stories and laughter. He has long crossed over. His first name was Danny and I will just leave that here. I sure do miss our talks in great length and him!

Oh, and one more thing that I have found. If you are going to design pants or bibs for hunting then make sure that the width of the calf area is enough to fit over snake boots please. Make sure that there is also a layer of thin insulation there too! Just because you are wearing snake boots does not mean the lower legs are protected from the cold. OK, off my soap box and on to the next subject…lol.

CALLS

Electronic and Mouth Calls

We will start with electronic calls simply because I do not use them which in turns leads to not having much knowledge on them. I do have an old FoxPro and an old Lohman CD player with lots of sound clips on them. I have dabbled with them from time to time but without success. It could be because they don't work in my area or I just don't have the knowledge to play the right scenario with them. Many and I mean many hunters have had and continue to have great success with these. I must admit that I am envious with this ability.

There are many good electronic calls out there on the market. I do believe that FoxPro is still leading the bandwagon. That company has been around for a very long time which plainly explains that they know their stuff when it comes to this product! So ,when hunters ask me which product or company they should seek out, it is hands down, my immediate recommendation Fox-Pro. I have no affiliation with them but I know what word on the streets among the many hunters that I have talked with over 30 years is this company. So, in closing on this topic, do your homework, talk to as many hunters that you can, research articles and

you will come up with what works for you in your areas that you hunt.

Mouth Calls are something I do know a thing or two about, so we will switch gears here. From the time I wanted to start learning about the coyotes and start targeting them for hunting, it was a mouth call that I picked up at a local sporting goods store. It was an open reed call. I wanted to learn the flexibility of this type from barking to howling and even female chirps. This in turn led me to purchase another brand and another.

All the calls I was buying were very high-pitched. They sounded nothing like our eastern coyotes. Ours were deeper tones, not the high pitched tones these calls were producing. I learned after hunting out west in later years that I was correct in my assessment on this topic.

The rabbit in distress calls were relatively all the same producing sound of distress. I still purchased different companies just to have a variety in my bag of tricks. With that said, it is a valuable piece of advice from someone who has been in it for a long time. Circe or Lohman was my all-time go to call for the rabbit distress. Very realistic in my humble opinion!

I will even take squeakers from some of my dog's toys that they chew out and put them to good use for distress calls. The Wiggly Squiggly Ball is a huge hit. They are inside of a cylinder in the ball. The waling sounds they produce are downright pitiful but yet perfect for distress.

We can't forget the squeakers that make perfect mouse squeaking sounds too that your fur children spit out! They are also a keeper when it comes to your bag of tricks!

So get creative and don't be afraid of have lots of options to choose from. Later, when I get to talking about scenarios, you will see that I use many of these sounds together.

I started seeing the benefits of the crow's knowledge early on so I knew I had to have a crow call. I went through many companies with that and settled on one. I listened carefully to what they were producing and discovered that many sounded like it was coming out of a tin can. Knowing what real time sound from my crows, was what helped me in that decision. It was a Madd call. I was still not 100% happy until I developed my own crow call, but it was usable for the time being.

This pretty much sums up my variety of sounds that I use and have them hanging off of my lanyard, readably available at any moment's time.

The most free gift of all is from all the winged ones...

As you have read in my stories the Crows are so important to predator hunting. They are my eyes of the forest. They are messengers of what is coming through the woods and where it is coming out at. If you just listen and watch them, they can tell you where your target has dropped down for you to go and retrieve.

If you go up there with a mindset of not hunting crows, they will not give you away, instead they will become your guides.

Like the dog toys I mentioned, this is yet another free tool for your bag of tricks. Just watch the reactions of all of the other animals out there and how they react to the crow's alarms.

There was one time that I had shot a coyote and it went into the woods. I knew it was a good hit. I called my tracker aka Husband and he went into the thick cover. There was a Crow that flew down and landed in the tree top of this pine. It was giving me a non-stop, alarming Kaw, over and over again.

My husband came back into the clearing and said he could not find it. The Crow was still sounding off so I said to him… Follow the Crow. He thought I was half nuts but listened to my advice and went back in to the tree where the Crow was perched on. Within a minute he hollered out that he found the coyote. As soon as he retrieved the coyote and started dragging it out, the crow flew off without another word.

Another incident was when I hit a coyote and it disappeared in the hay field. I drove all over that field, at least I thought I did and could not find it at all. Morning sun came up and the crows were flying around. One in particular kept on dive bombing over a particular spot in that hay field. Flying back and forth it kept on diving. So after some thought, I hopped on my four wheeler and drove out to that spot. There was the coyote laying there.

Another time was a coyote that went into the corn field after I shot it. Again, the crows found that by dive bombing and circling over the same spot. Never dismiss the ones that have the birds' eye view of helping you to see what you can't find on your own. They have taught me so well in this sport. I will never doubt them.

Another one is the woodpecker. They have a piercing sound when they sense a predator coming close to them as they fly off. If they are happily pecking in the woods then all is good, but the minute you hear their alarm and fly off, you had better look around the bottom of that tree for what scared them out. Nine times out of ten it is some sort of a predator as in a Coyote or Bobcat. The one out of 10 times could be another human walking through

Now Blue-Jays are, in my opinion a spazzy kind of bird, but like the Crows and the Woodpecker, they have the defense alarm as well when danger is presenting itself. So, learn their language and be aware of the change in surroundings of where they just flew out of.

LET'S TALK SCENARIOS

The reason that I have been so particular on different brands of calls is because I want it to sound real life as if I was out in the woods, the same thing goes for scenarios too! If you have ever gone to any of my seminars you will always hear me say… "Keep It Real!" So, if you don't hear those sequences playing out in the woods, don't try it in your calling. I go for the most realistic sounding calls to the most realistic play of sounds as if the entire scene had just happened in the field or woods.

Springtime, when the coyotes are working on their den site before pups and after, I focus more on the food sounds. So early morning when I know the coyotes are going back to their dens, I will set out a turkey decoy. The first sound I use at daylight will be my Crow call. I use lots of chatter because that is what the Crows do just starting out their day.

Then I will start clucking on my slate call as if I am a lost turkey from a flock. I might throw in a gobble. More Crow vocalizations and then get quiet for about a minute or two. If no immediate reaction I will start clucking again on the slate call and add more Crow sounds.

This subtle play of sounds can be immediate reaction or take up to 30 minutes of calling to pique the interest of a coyote and bring him in. But it is well worth it and very little effort on your part. I have had pairs of coyotes come in with this scenario. If you know what fields the turkeys are in right before they go to roost at night, this scenario is also perfect to use at that time when the coyotes are just getting ready to start their hunts at night.

A word of warning though, you might ruin or lose some turkey decoys so I would invest in some back up, cheap ones!

Summertime, whether it be morning, noon or night, I start to add in the distressed fawn bleats. This bleating sound will go on for up 10 minutes with some Crow alarm calls in between as if to say, I am alone and need help. This scenario has been a 50/50 success for me. But it has been beneficial and is a change up from other routines hunting in the same area over and over again. You always have to be willing to change things up. Coyotes are not dumb. That is also why I have several different brands of calls too, remember that. A slightly different tone can increase your success rate.

If you want to get in good with farmers and their land for hunting I would highly suggest groundhog hunting. Once you shoot a groundhog, just come back in the evening and watch the coyotes come right in for the meal. There must be a specific smell that the groundhogs give off, other than obviously death of course, because it has always worked for me. So offer up to the farmer to take out groundhogs and be able to hunt coyotes at night too, a deal package.

Fall, I will start using Crow, and Coyote vocalizations, with less emphasis on food source sounds. My reasoning behind this is because, coyotes are moving in after being kicked out of their dens, males starting to look for mates and they are starting to think about getting their Groove on, so to speak.

So this is when I bring the entire kitchen sink of sounds to the playground. From barks to howls, to chirps to growls, distress to mating sounds to every kind of coyote vocalization I can do, I will throw out there. Remembering that no matter what, to still keeping it real, even in time sequences. I do not go on and on with these sounds. I pick a couple of sounds, wait for about 30-40 seconds then add in a response type of answer in a different direction and so on. Get quiet after about a minute or two of calling, then silent for about another 5 minutes. Then I come up with a different scenario and do it again.

Keep in mind that these are MY WAYS of doing this and they may not work for you in your hunting areas. I tell people that they should watch as many videos, read lots of articles and listen to a lot of seminars and pick and choose out of all you learned, what might work for you in your area. Also, don't treat everything you read or hear as the gospel. Some might be trying to sell you a call or something hunting related. Always wear your BS Detectors!!! Lol

About the beginning of December until the end of February, I focus mainly on Female Estrus Chirps and barks and male vocalizations. With the males I will do a lot of fight scenes between male coyotes over just hearing an Estrus Chirp or female bark. Sometimes I will add in some soft whimpering and enticing sounds from a female too. In my opinion and what I have witnessed during this period is that the coyotes don't care about responding to food sounds, let's face it, they have other things on their mind.

One last thing that I wanted to pass on to you is that from May until about middle of July the coyotes will be more on the quiet side. This is because they don't want to give away their den sights. So, although you may not get any vocal responses, pay attention closely. They sneak in quietly and show up when you least expect it. So, don't dismiss this as nothing is responding to your calls. This could also be said about over called coyotes too.

I hope I have given you some tips that can help you in your area. Keep at it… shoot straight… never give up!

CHAPTER 17

RAMBLINGS FROM THIS OLE CROW
MY JOURNEY

November 7ᵗʰ 2020 is the Best Night in such a very long time for me. As I sit here in my Cabin on the Greens, a flood of emotions run through me like a raging river cascading down a mountain side.

This date, InfraRed, Thermal and Night Vision became legal for predator hunters in the state of Pennsylvania. This is the day I have been working so hard to get to. It will be 4 years in January 2021 that will mark the first speech I gave to the Pennsylvania Game Commissioners about my quest for this equipment to be legalized. Such a long journey it has been.

It was a journey filled with Game Commissioners, State Representatives, Senators, Organizations, Powerful People and even my share of haters along the way. I have learned from the Liars, Death Threats, Clicks and Game Players more than I could have possibly even imagined at times. They have been my fuel to keep on burning and turning and most importantly keep going forward with my passion.

I have also been so blessed to have in my corner the Genuine Supporters, Legislators, Organizations and thousands upon thousands of Predator Hunters that wanted this change and made me feel the strength to see this through. My Dad's words were right there in my mind telling me to "Stand in My Truth" at every turn in this game. Unfortunately, this was a Game that needed to be played and somedays I was just sick emotionally seeing how I had to act and proceed to get this to the finish line.

I have lost so much of myself over these past few years. I have been so driven and focused at the end goal. That might not sound so bad but it was in a way for me, that I stopped laughing, unless I was playing the game. I had taken on not only my passion, but the pressure of feeling like I could not fail all of these hunters that are counting on me.

That weight I carried on my shoulders was overpowering at times, not that in any way they made me do it… that was just the way I saw what had to be done. I was focused beyond belief and driven to the point that I ate, slept and drank this Bill!!!

My family felt like they were walking on egg shells around me. It was 24 hours a day this Bill and what I had to do next or the next appointment I had to go to or the next speech I had to write or the next presentation I had to do. That was my life for almost 4 years. It was a crazy and mixed up kind of mindset. My own family didn't know how or what to say to me. I was not ME.

I did not like the person I had become. I remember the countless times I would say to them... bear with me... we are almost to the finish line. And just like that, another wrench would be thrown into the works... another setback after setback and then a new plan would have to be thought of to make it get back on track!

I was both the Firestarter and the Fire Extinguisher in this crazy house! It was a constant Roller Coaster and I hate Roller Coasters... I wanted off so many times BUT I was going to see this thing finished and signed on the dotted line!!!

I wanted just one thing that I could truly feel Proud of in my life before my time was up... I just wanted one thing that I know in my heart and spirit that My Dad would Be Proud of me... I wanted all of the Haters and the nay-sayers to eat Crow... and I wanted my once started Passion to become a reality for not just myself but for all the Predator Hunters of this State!!!

So, tonight is about Reflections of My Journey. The long winding road, sometimes deep with potholes and cliffs. Tonight, I sit back and turn on my InfraRed equipment and begin to glass the fields and shed some tears. I did this... I say to myself... I am Proud of Myself... It is finally finished...

the PA Farm B___ ___ ___y impedi-
ment to expanded hunting opportunities for
families) has asked for in the past. The bill
has been referred to the Senate Game &
Fisheries Committee.

A co-sponsor memo is being circu-
lated by Representative Parke Wentling (R-
Crawford/Erie). Wentling's bill, if passed,
would remove the prohibition of night vision and infrared devices so they could be
regulated by the Game Commission for use
in hunting predators. PFSC recently con-
tacted all House members urging them to
sign on as co-sponsors. As of July 23rd
there were 29 co-sponsors on this letter.
bill should be officially introduced very
on.

Any further legislation affecting hunt
fishing and trapping is not likely t

PA State Representative, Clint Owlett

L-R, Josh First, PA Senator Gene Yaw, me and Harold Daub.

Capital Building in Harrisburg, PA.

Wayne LaPierre, NRA.

My Journey... HB1188, the Bill that changed the law for All Predator Hunters in PA to lift the restrictions on the use of Thermal and Infrared optics for hunting predators at night.

For the first time in such a long time, I am remembering how I used to feel when I first started hunting. I am hearing Nature's Symphony. I am listening to coyotes singing off in the far distance. I am feeling the enjoyment of seeing all of the deer right out in front of me while I am within 25 yards in their own playground and they don't even know that I'm here.

For the first time while I sit here...

... there is NO more Stress

... NO more Pressure from myself or others of letting us down

... NO more appointments to be made

... NO more strategies to think up

... NO more moves to make in this game!

I am tying a fine bow on this package and moving forward... with family first!!!

I will treasure my times in the Outdoors like I used to. I will remember the animals and all they have taught me. I will Breathe as I live in the dark nights with my equipment enjoying "The Hunt!"

Thank You All for Believing in me even when I didn't believe myself... Thank You, Lord! For without you in my life, I would have not gotten through this!!!

THROUGH THE YEARS

Photo Gallery

Fun Times always at Bass Pro with Greg Bulkley and Byron Conners. Also rewarding were the seminars I gave for women in the outdoors.

Bob Foulkrod — A Man... A Legend, whom I have great respect for. Thank You Bob for your friendship and all the years of advice!

Fan holding my first book, Coyote Hunting Farm Style.

One of Countless shows with my Daughter Jamie and me.

A Badass picture taken with 2 other hunters getting ready for a Coyote hunt, all equipped with our NiteSite Infrared equipment up in New York.

Shirley Grenoble, Joanie Haidle and me at a weekend turkey hunt.

A group of Veterans at my house waiting to go coyote hunting after a long day of doe hunting. Only one made the nighttime hunt... didn't you, Bryan!

Ladies Hog Hunt hosted by Nancy Jo Adams and Racknine Outdoors down South

Special Friends made along the way.

Made in United States
Orlando, FL
07 December 2024

55098202R00085